INTO THE
WORD

Other Books by Anne Graham Lotz

The Magnificent Obsession

The Vision of His Glory

God's Story

Daily Light

Just Give Me Jesus

Heaven: My Father's House

My Jesus Is ... Everything

Life Is Just Better with Jesus

Pursuing MORE of Jesus

Why? Trusting God When You Don't Understand

The Joy of My Heart

I Saw The LORD

INTO THE
WORD

52 LIFE-CHANGING BIBLE STUDIES
for INDIVIDUALS *and* GROUPS

ANNE
GRAHAM
LOTZ

ZONDERVAN.com/
AUTHORTRACKER
follow your favorite authors

ZONDERVAN

Into the Word
Copyright © 2010 by Anne Graham Lotz

This title is also available as a Zondervan ebook.
Visit www.zondervan.com/ebooks.

This title is also available in a Zondervan audio edition.
Visit www.zondervan.fm.

Requests for information should be addressed to:

Zondervan, *Grand Rapids, Michigan 49530*

ISBN 978-0-310-32538-3

Published in association with the literary agency of Alive Communications, Inc., 7680 Goddard St., Suite 200, Colorado Springs, CO 80920. www.alivecommunications.com

Cover design: Rob Monacelli
Interior design: Ben Fetterley

Printed in the United States of America.

10 11 12 13 14 15 16 17 18 • 22 21 20 19 18 17 16 15 14 13 12 11 10 9 8 7 6 5 4

To

Miss A. Wetherell Johnson

Founder of Bible Study Fellowship
Who taught me how to get into the Word

Contents

PART 3

March — HARDSHIP

PART 4

April — GRACE

PART 5

May — PRAYER

PART 6

June — WISDOM

PART 7

July — REVIVAL

PART 8

August — REST

PART 9

September — INVOLVEMENT

PART 10

October — TIME

PART 11

November — GRATITUDE

PART 12

December — CHRIST

The pressures of day-to-day responsibility, the news of crisis after crisis in our world, the problems I face within my family or ministry, can have an unsettling effect. I find that my spirit tends to get overwhelmed, and, without being able to pinpoint the specific cause, I can feel burdened on the inside.

I have drawn encouragement from the fact that Jesus' disciples also experienced problems, pressures, and unwelcome news. In Mark 6 they seemed to go through an emotional roller coaster when they were bombarded with the horror of the brutal beheading of John the Baptist, the thrill of experiencing the power of God to change lives through their ministry, and the exhaustion of having no time to even eat because of the demands placed on them. Jesus, understanding their emotional, spiritual, and physical needs of the moment, said, "Come with Me by yourselves." I have discovered by personal experience that His solution for the disciples of old is His same solution for disciples today. You and I are invited to draw aside and spend time with Him.

The catch? We need to *have* time to *spend* time. And if you are like me, you don't have a minute to spare. So I have to make the time. To be honest, there are days of travel, or speaking, or illness, or ministry business, or days when I just succumb to the tyranny of the urgent and miss spending a few moments with Him. Instead of wrestling with the guilt of failing to achieve my goal of daily time with Him, I have a rather simple solution. I make sure that at least once a week, I draw aside with Jesus. It's like setting my spiritual compass. That time of retreat keeps the "needle" of my heart and mind focused on Him, regardless of what happens during the week.

So ...

If you too are bombarded by pressures, problems, or unwelcome news ...

If your spirit is overwhelmed within you ...

If you know you should spend time in God's Word ...

If you long to draw aside with Jesus for a time of intimate fellowship ...

If you feel spiritually dry because you have allowed your work to come before your worship ...

If you just need some help in studying your Bible ...

Then this book has been designed for you.

A total of fifty-two Bible studies are laid out in these pages, one for each week of the year. I invite you to set your spiritual compass. Draw aside with Jesus by using these studies to get *Into the Word*.

Anne Graham Lotz

January

BEGINNINGS

A Second Chance

I once heard a speaker ask what we thought God expected of us. Mentally I answered, "Righteousness, holiness, love for God and my neighbor." He repeated his question, so I continued my list, "Bible reading, prayer, obedience, service." But then he stated, to my stunned amazement, "All God ever expects of you is failure."

I had to resist the temptation to raise my hand, wave it wildly, and exclaim, "I can do that! I can live up to God's expectations! I know I can fail!" But before I could blurt it out, the speaker said, "But He has given you the Holy Spirit so that you need never fail."

As we begin the new year, have you stopped making resolutions because of repeated failure to keep the old ones? Do your past failures discourage you in the present and paralyze you for the future? Then join me in praising the God who expects us in our flesh to fail, but who is also the God of the second chance!

Describe Peter's failure in Matthew 16:13 – 23; 26:31 – 45, 69 – 75; John 18:10 – 11.

In what way have you failed as a parent? Sibling? Spouse? Friend? Church member? Christian witness? Describe your feelings after failure.

How do you think Peter felt after his repeated failures to be a disciple?

Read John 21:1 – 19

RECALLED AFTER FAILURE — John 21:1 – 8

What did fishing represent to Peter? See Matthew 4:18 – 20.

Why do you think Peter decided to go back to fishing in John 21:3?

What similarities are there between Peter's fishing experience before he was a disciple in Luke 5:4 – 7 and after the resurrection in John 21:3 – 6?

What do you think Jesus was trying to teach Peter? Consider John 15:5; Romans 7:18; 1 Peter 1:18 – 19; Galatians 5:1.

If your repeated failure has led you to go back to an old way of life, how has God set you up for a recall to discipleship?

REFILLED AFTER FAILURE — John 21:9–14

In John 21:9, what did Peter find when he swam to shore?

What did Jesus tell Peter and the other disciples to do in verse 10?

What were the two sources for the fish that made up Peter's breakfast in verses 6 – 13? Where did the bread come from?

What does this teach you about being spiritually fed and satisfied? See John 6:35, 51, 57 – 58, 63; 2 Timothy 2:15; 1 Peter 2:2; Psalm 19:9 – 11; Colossians 3:16; Romans 15:4.

Especially after failure, what are you doing to "feed" yourself? To be fed by others?

RESTORED AFTER FAILURE — John 21:15–17

What similarities are there between Peter's denial of Jesus in Luke 22:54 – 62 and his confession of Him in John 21:15 – 17? What are the differences?

If the similarities were intentional, how do you think the interaction with Jesus in verses 15 – 17 helped to restore Peter to discipleship?

Instead of dwelling on past failure, what confession did Jesus provoke from Peter? What command did Jesus give Peter in verse 15? Verse 16? Verse 17? Explain what each command means. Give an application of each for your own life.

Who are the hungry "sheep" in your life? See Mark 6:34; Isaiah 53:6; Luke 15:3 – 7; 1 Peter 2:25.

What is the difference between a sheep and a lamb? Who are the hungry lambs in your life?

Give practical ways you can feed the sheep and the lambs.

What are some ways that you tend sheep? See Hebrews 13:1 – 3; 1 Peter 3:8; 1 John 3:16 – 18.

What is your present attitude toward Jesus, regardless of past failures? Do you love Him? Do you really love Jesus? Do you even like Him? If so, what is the obvious conclusion from what He said?

Read the following verses: Jeremiah 3:22; Ezekiel 37:23; Hosea 14:4; 1 Peter 1:1 – 3; 1 Corinthians 1:26 – 31. How do they encourage you?

REFOCUSED AFTER FAILURE — John 21:18 – 19

According to church tradition, Peter died by crucifixion. Relate what Jesus said to Peter in John 21:18 – 19 to what Jesus said to all disciples in Matthew 16:24 – 25; Mark 8:34 – 38; Luke 9:23 – 26.

How did Paul describe his own "crucifixion" in Galatians 2:20?

Relate the ambitions, actions, words, and thoughts of a physically dead man to the spiritual death of self.

What do you think "taking up the cross" in your life means? See 1 Corinthians 6:19 – 20; 1 Peter 2:24; Romans 8:12 – 14; John 12:24 – 25.

What command did Jesus issue twice to Peter in John 21:19 – 22? What does this command mean for your own discipleship? See 1 Peter 2:21; Romans 15:5 – 6; Mark 10:17 – 21; John 10:14, 27 – 28; Matthew 19:27 – 29; Luke 9:57 – 62.

Does anything distort your focus on the cross? Does anything hinder you from following Christ? Name it and put it out of your life.

As you gratefully accept a second chance after failure, which of these verses is most meaningful to you for the new year: Hebrews 12:1 – 3; Philippians 3:12 – 14; Romans 8:1 – 4; 2 Corinthians 5:17 – 21; Revelation 21:3 – 5?

During this new year, let your life, like Peter's, bear witness that our God is Lord of the slim chance, the fat chance, the no chance ... and the second chance!

Answer His recall to discipleship now. Tune your ears to His voice as you read His Word and ask Him to refill you. Open your heart to be restored in love for Him and in service to Him. Then refocus your entire life on Jesus as you follow Him. He will lead you to a cross. Deny yourself and take it up. But don't forget, after the cross comes the resurrection, the power, the glory, and the crown!

In all of human history, few names are greater than that of Abraham — the father of the Jews, the father of the Arabs, and the father of faith for Christians. Yet Abraham's life, again and again, was marked by failure. The reason we associate Abraham with faith and friendship with God is that when he failed, he didn't quit. He got right with God, then kept pressing forward. He began again.

In what ways have you failed? Have you failed as a disciple of Jesus Christ? Are you tempted to quit? The new year is a wonderful time to begin again.

Read Genesis 12:1 – 13:4

AFTER THE CHOICE TO PURSUE KNOWING GOD

From the following verses, describe who Abraham was when God first called him. See Genesis 11:26 – 27; Joshua 24:2 – 4; Acts 7:2.

Of all the people living on planet Earth at the time, why do you think God called Abraham? See Genesis 18:18 – 19; Deuteronomy 7:7 – 8; Proverbs 8:17; Jeremiah 29:13.

Relate Abraham's calling to your calling. Consider the following verses: Ephesians 1:4; 2 Thessalonians 2:13; 1 Peter 1:2; 2:9.

The choice is personal

Count the personal pronouns in Genesis 12:1 – 3. What do they tell you about God's call to Abraham and Abraham's choice to respond?

Read Matthew 4:19 and 16:24 – 26, inserting your own name for the personal pronouns.

When did you reject living an apathetic, complacent, pew-warming type of Christian life and make the choice to pursue knowing God by your own experience? Give the approximate date and describe the circumstances surrounding your choice.

The choice is powerful

How did Abraham's choice change his life? Relate this choice to John 3:36; 5:24.

How did Abraham's choice enrich his life? See Genesis 12:2 – 3. Relate this to John 10:10; Ephesians 1:3.

What veiled promise did God give to Abraham in the last phrase of Genesis 12:3? See Galatians 3:16; John 8:56 – 58. How is this promise given to you in a spiritual sense? See 1 John 3:2; 2 Corinthians 3:18.

How has the choice to pursue God changed your life? Enriched your life?

AFTER THE COMMITMENT TO PURSUE KNOWING GOD

The commitment to walk

Restate the command God gave to Abraham in Genesis 12:1. Give the three phrases that indicate Abraham's obedience to that command in Genesis 12:4 – 5.

How old was Abraham when he followed through on his commitment to pursue God?

Do you think you are too old to begin a lifetime commitment? Too young? Too busy? Too poor? Why do you feel as you do?

What do you learn from the following people who also walked with God? See Genesis 5:21 – 24 with Hebrews 11:5. Also Genesis 6:9 with Hebrews 11:7; Luke 24:13 – 27.

What special promise is given in 1 John 1:7 to those who walk with God?

The commitment to worship

What do you think the altar could represent in Genesis 12:7 – 8?

In what way could you build an "altar" today? See 1 Chronicles 16:29; Romans 12:1; Matthew 6:5 – 6; Psalm 63:1; Habakkuk 2:1.

How does God desire to be worshiped today? See John 4:23 – 24. Does your worship satisfy His desire?

AFTER THE COLLAPSE OF THE PURSUIT TO KNOW GOD

We wander

What circumstance seemed to trigger Abraham's wandering away from where God had led him? How can this same circumstance occur spiritually in our lives?

Was Abraham operating under God's direction? What decision have you made without prayer?

What phrase indicates Abraham thought going to Egypt was a small, insignificant, temporary decision?

We worry

What was Abraham worried about? Were his fears legitimate? Why or why not?

What are you worried about? What does God say about worry in Matthew 6:25 – 34; Philippians 4:6?

We do wrong

How did Abraham's worry lead him into wrongdoing? How has your worry led you to sin?

Describe the suffering that resulted from Abraham's sin. Who has suffered as a result of your sin?

Do you think sin is ever confined exclusively to one person or does it affect others? Give examples from your own life.

Have you ever been rebuked by a non-Christian for something you should not have done? Describe how you felt.

Which phrases indicate that Abraham profited from his sin? Do you think the wealth Abraham acquired in Egypt was a sign of God's blessing? See Genesis 13:5 – 7; 16:1 – 6.

Has sin led to suffering that has led to shame that has led to a substitute for God's blessing in your life? Are you painfully aware of your failures in the past?

Return

What phrase indicates Abraham was searching for God?

After leaving Egypt, where did Abraham end up? What was the significance of this place in Abraham's life?

What do you think the altar represented to Abraham at this stage? See Isaiah 6:5 – 7; 44:22; 55:7; Jeremiah 3:22; 24:7; Colossians 1:20; 2:14.

Repent

Repentance means to turn around, to stop sinning, to change your mind. What evidence is there that Abraham truly repented?

As you choose to return to the cross and repent of your sin, write a prayer. See Psalm 51 for help.

As you return to the cross in repentance of sin, give phrases that encourage you from 1 John 1:7 – 9; Ephesians 1:7; Psalm 103:12; 32:1 – 5.

Has your whole journey collapsed into miserable failure? Then come back to the cross. Come back to Jesus. Celebrate this new year by beginning again.

Going Deeper

Several summers ago while our family was vacationing at the beach, I got up early to meet the Lord for a few moments of quiet before the family awakened. As I sat on the porch, watching the sun come up over the ocean and listening to the gentle crash of the waves on the shore, the Lord seemed to whisper to my heart, "What do you see?" I looked more closely at the scene before me and answered Him in my spirit, "I see little sandpipers running along the edge of the water, making sure they keep out of reach of the waves and don't even get their feet wet. I see the skimmers flying down the beach, skimming the surface of the water with their long beaks. I see seagulls standing in the tide up to their knees. And I see the pelicans that circle, then dive headfirst into the waves, coming up with fish they seem to swallow whole."

Then the Lord seemed to say to me, "The Bible is like the ocean, and the people who read My Word are very much like those birds. Some will dance around the Scriptures, not really wanting to step in and get their feet wet in Bible study. They are satisfied to just listen to their preacher or Bible teacher tell them what the Bible says. Others will read their Bibles, just skimming the surface for facts and information. Some will get in knee-deep, reading the Bible each day with a devotional or commentary close by for reference. And then there are some, like the pelicans, who dive in over their heads, going deep in Bible study, applying and living out what they learn. Which bird are you most like?"

I answered with wholehearted passion, "Lord, I'm not sure which one I am from Your perspective. But I know which one I want to be. Please take me deeper into Your Word." And He has.

Which bird most accurately describes you? Would you resolve to be more like the pelican and go deeper into the Word?

Read Revelation 2:12 – 17

The ancient city of Pergamum was in what is now Turkey. Built on a rather flat plain, it was dominated by one hill located at the center, on top of which was one of the seven wonders of the ancient world: a spectacular white marble temple to Zeus. It also had a medical complex and a university that housed more than 200,000 volumes.

A church had been planted in the city, with the high hopes of making an impact on this major religious, medical, and intellectual center with the gospel.

GOING DEEPER AS YOU LOOK INTO HIS WORD

How does Jesus identify Himself to the church in Pergamum? Read Revelation 2:12.

On what was He trying to get them to focus? See Ephesians 6:17; Hebrews 4:12; Revelation 19:11 – 13.

From the following verses, give phrases that indicate He wants us to focus on the same thing: 2 Timothy 1:13 – 14; 2:2, 15; 3:14 – 17; Hebrews 12:2.

Does anything hinder you from focusing on God's living and written Word for yourself? What could you do about that? Apply Hebrews 12:1 to your daily discipline of Bible reading.

What will you do now to make sure that by next year you will be deeper into the Word than you are today?

For what did Jesus commend the church in Pergamum in Revelation 2:13?

Give phrases from the following verses that reveal God knows "where you live" and how faithful you are to Him: Psalm 139:1 – 4, 23; 142:3; Job 23:10; John 1:48; 2:25; 4:29; 10:14.

What did Jesus have against the church in Pergamum? Without your knowing the details of who the Balaamites and Nicolaitans were, what does Jesus imply that they did? See Revelation 2:14 – 15.

How is it possible for a church leader or member to entice others to sin? Give examples from the following verses: Acts 5:1 – 11; 2 Timothy 3:5 – 9; 1 Corinthians 3:1 – 4; 5:9 – 11; 1 John 2:9, 15 – 16; Revelation 2:20.

What does Jesus tell the church members — not just the false teachers within the church — to do?

Do you think God holds us accountable for the church leadership we place ourselves under? Explain.

What are we to do to protect ourselves from this kind of deception and temptation? See 1 John 4:1 – 3; 1 Corinthians 15:33; 2 Timothy 3:16 – 17; 2 Corinthians 6:14 – 17; 11:13 – 15; Ephesians 6:10 – 18. Based on the verses above, how susceptible are you to deception — from within the church?

Do you think, because of our sophistication and knowledge, that we can stand in judgment over God's Word? Why or why not?

How do Revelation 2:16 and 19:11 – 16 reveal that God's Word stands in judgment over us?

GOING DEEPER AS YOU LISTEN TO HIS WORD

Do you think it is possible to read God's Word without really "hearing" what the Spirit has to say? See Revelation 2:17. What promises are given to those who have listened to what He has to say?

Describe "manna" from the following verses: Exodus 16:4, 31; John 6:31.

How was the manna hidden? See Exodus 16:31 – 33; Hebrews 9:2 – 4.

What did manna symbolize? See Deuteronomy 8:3; John 6:32 – 35.

What do you think Jesus meant when He promised to give "hidden manna" to the one who goes deeper into His Word? See Psalm 119:18; Luke 24:45; Matthew 11:27; John 14:21.

The church in Pergamum refused to go deeper into God's Word. Instead of making an impact on the world, the world made an impact on the church. Several years ago I visited the ruins of the old city. The ancient church was actually attached to a pagan temple. It became irrelevant, powerless, and, in the end, nonexistent.

Are you listening to what the Spirit is saying? Look ahead to the new year. If all church members were like you, would the church be more like the world? Or, would the church be more powerful in its witness — making an impact on our generation for the kingdom of God — because it would be deeper into the Word?

February

LOVE

Give Him Your Heart

Sending valentines in February is a traditional way to celebrate. To whom will you send a valentine this year? Who will send one to you? Do you save the really special ones? The ones that include a personal note or express the intimate feelings of the sender?

In the first century, the church at Ephesus received a letter from Jesus that could be thought of as a valentine. While it was not the traditional kind, it was one that was kept because of its personal nature and because of the revelation it gives us of the sender's heart.

Read Revelation 2:1 – 7

LOVE'S FOCUS

Name some of the Christian leaders God sent to Ephesus. See Acts 18:19 – 21, 24 – 28; 1 Corinthians 16:8 – 9; 1 Timothy 1:2 – 4; 2 Timothy 1:16 – 18.

Whose leadership have you been under, either in your church or through books, CDs, or other materials?

Do you think it is possible to focus more on a person who has helped you grow in your faith than on God? Explain.

Is access to great spiritual leadership a guarantee that you will grow in your love for God? See Daniel 9:6 – 7.

On whom does Jesus immediately place the focus in Revelation 2:1? See also Revelation 1:13, 16, 18, 20.

+ What does this teach you?

Using Revelation 1:20, put the description of Jesus in Revelation 2:1 in your own words. (Note: Angels are messengers of God. Based on Matthew 28:19 – 20 and Acts 1:8, all of us are "angels" in this sense of the word.)

+ Apply this particular description of Jesus to your life.

+ Think carefully. Where is your focus?

LOVE'S FERVOR

From Revelation 2:2 – 3, 6, list all the things that the Ephesian Christians were doing.

Why do you think they were so busy?

Relate the activity of the Ephesian Christians to John 14:23; 21:15 – 17; James 1:25; 2:17; 1 John 4:11; 1 Thessalonians 1:3.

How busy are you in service to God? List the various Christian and church-related activities you're involved in.

Why are you busy for God? See Colossians 3:23 – 24.

LOVE'S FAILURE

What did Jesus rebuke the Ephesian Christians for in Revelation 2:4? How did He rebuke Israel for the same thing? See Isaiah 29:13.

Describe what you think "first love" is. For help, see Song of Songs 3:1 – 4.

Give phrases from the following verses that underscore either the priority God places on our love for Him or how we should love Him: Deuteronomy 6:5; 30:6, 19 – 20; Joshua 22:5; 23:11; Psalm 31:23; 69:34 – 36; 116:1 – 2; Hosea 4:1; 6:4; Matthew 22:36 – 37; John 14:15; 15:9; 1 Corinthians 2:9; 16:22; Ephesians 6:24; James 1:12; Proverbs 8:17; 1 John 4:19.

Do you think the Ephesian Christians deliberately forsook their love for Jesus, gradually drifted from it, or wearily buried it in busyness? Why?

How could the fervency of their love actually have contributed to their falling away from it?

What work for God have you put before your worship of Him?

LOVE'S FAITH

What three things did Jesus command the Ephesian Christians to do in Revelation 2:5 to regain their first love?

To remember

Do you love Jesus? Passionately, fervently, obediently, constantly? If not, can you remember a time when you did? In Psalm 42:1 – 4, how does the psalmist express love for God?

Make a list of things you can remember that God has done for you and of times when your relationship with Him was intimately personal. See Deuteronomy 8:2; Job 29:1 – 5; Song of Songs 3:1 – 2; Ephesians 2:11 – 13.

To repent

Define in your own words what it means to repent.

What happens when we repent, from God's perspective and from ours? See Jeremiah 15:19; Ezekiel 18:30 – 32; Luke 13:3; Acts 3:19; 8:22 – 23; 26:19 – 20; Revelation 3:19.

List the sins from which you need to repent, beginning with falling away from your love for God. See Hosea 14:1 – 2.

To return

What "first things" do you think the Ephesian Christians needed to return to in Revelation 2:5? See Joel 2:12 – 14; Zechariah 1:3; Malachi 3:6 – 10; Acts 20:17 – 37; 1 Corinthians 1:18.

What were you doing when you first loved the Lord that you are not doing now? What do you need to do to put that back into your life?

What were you not doing when you first loved the Lord that you are doing now? What will you do today to put that out of your life?

What do you think is symbolized by the lampstand? See Matthew 5:14 – 16; Revelation 1:20. From Revelation 2:5, write the warning Jesus gives to those who do not regain their first love.

What spiritual principles can you draw from Revelation 2:1 – 6? See also 1 Samuel 16:7; Psalm 51:17; Proverbs 4:23; Mark 12:30.

To whom was Jesus speaking in Revelation 2:7?

What two different kinds of ears can God's people have? See Psalm 40:6; Proverbs 18:15; 20:12; Ezekiel 12:2; Isaiah 50:4 – 5; Acts 7:51; 28:27; 2 Timothy 4:3 – 4. Which do you have?

In Revelation 2:7, what promise did Jesus give to those who overcome their lovelessness toward Him?

What is represented by the tree of life? See Genesis 2:9; 3:22, 24; Revelation 22:1 – 2, 14.

How did Jesus describe the life He gives? See John 10:10; 17:3.

What do you think is meant by His promise in Revelation 2:7 that we can eat from the tree?

What or where is paradise? See Luke 23:43; 2 Corinthians 12:2 – 4.

If Jesus' promise is that those who love Him with a "first love" can eat from the tree of life in the paradise of God now, what does this mean for you?

Jesus desires your love more than all of your service and obedience combined. Don't put your work before your worship; give Him your heart!

His Nearness in My Loneliness

Teenage suicide victims, alcoholics, drug addicts, divorcees, widows and widowers, singles, juvenile delinquents, prison inmates, cancer victims, and the eleven disciples of Jesus on the Thursday evening before the crucifixion — they all have something in common. What is it? It's an overwhelming sense of loneliness.

In our overpopulated world, with people ...

+ walking on crowded sidewalks,
+ riding crowded buses,
+ living in crowded housing,
+ driving on crowded streets,
+ shopping in crowded malls,
+ vacationing in crowded resorts,
+ backpacking in crowded parks,
+ eating in crowded restaurants,
+ working in crowded offices,
+ dying in crowded hospitals

... many are desperately lonely. The dictionary defines loneliness as being without companionship; a feeling of desolation; depressed at being alone.

When have you felt lonely — even in a crowd? Desolate? Alone, without companionship, to the point you were depressed? Does your loneliness stem from the fact that you feel unknown? Misunderstood? Ignored? Then you need Jesus — and you need more of His nearness in your loneliness because Jesus knows you. He understands you. And you have His undivided attention through the person of the Holy Spirit.

Read John 16:5 – 16

In John 16:5 – 7, why did the disciples need comfort? What do you think they were feeling?

Comfort of His person

What names does John 16:5 – 16 use in speaking of the Holy Spirit? What does this teach you about the Holy Spirit?

What do the following passages tell us about names in Scripture? See Genesis 32:27 – 28; Matthew 1:21; 16:17 – 18.

List four names for the Holy Spirit from John 16:6 – 7 (KJV); John 16:13; 14:26.

Give the dictionary definition for the key word of each name; then write, in your own words, how the key word describes an aspect of the Holy Spirit's work or character.

Assign each of the following verses to one of the names of the Holy Spirit and apply each verse to your own life: 2 Timothy 3:16; 1 Peter 1:15 – 16; 2 Corinthians 1:3 – 4; James 1:5.

Which of His names is most meaningful to you? Why?

Comfort of His presence

What promise did Jesus give His disciples in John 16:7; 14:16 – 17? How does His promise differ from the Old Testament experience of the Holy Spirit in Numbers 11:25; Judges 14:6; 1 Samuel 16:13; Psalm 51:11?

From Acts 2:1 – 21, describe how Jesus kept His promise.

Although Pentecost, like the birth, death, and resurrection of Jesus, was a historical event never to be repeated, when does the Holy Spirit come into a person's life? See Acts 2:38; Ephesians 1:13 – 14. Once you have received the Holy Spirit, according to these verses, is His presence temporary or permanent?

HIS NEARNESS BRINGS CHANGE

Compare Genesis 1:2 with Genesis 1:3 – 31. What role do you think the Holy Spirit had at creation? Do you think His power is less today?

He changes me

From the following verses, how does the Holy Spirit bring about change in our lives? See 2 Corinthians 3:18; Romans 7:6; 8:5 – 6; 1 Corinthians 2:12 – 13; Ephesians 6:17 – 18; Philippians 3:3; 1 Thessalonians 1:4 – 6; 2 Thessalonians 2:13; Titus 3:5; Jude 20; Revelation 2:29.

What command does Ephesians 4:29 – 31 give us in reference to the Holy Spirit? Explain this command in your own words. If we grieve only for those we genuinely care about and love, what does this imply about the Holy Spirit's relationship with every believer?

What command does God give us in Ephesians 5:18? Give phrases from Ephesians 5:1 – 2, 10, 15, 17, 20 that help us understand how to obey this command.

From Galatians 5:22 – 25 and Acts 4:31, what evidence of the Holy Spirit's filling should others be able to see in our lives?

He changes others

According to Jesus in John 16:8 – 11, how does the Holy Spirit change others? Based on these verses, do you think guilt is a good or a bad thing? Why?

The Holy Spirit will convict the world of guilt in regard to three things. What are they? Pray that the Holy Spirit would do this in the lives of the unsaved people on your prayer list.

If the Holy Spirit's responsibility is to convict the world of guilt and to convince the world of truth, what would be the most effective way to bring about change in another person's life?

From John 18:15 – 18, 25 – 27, describe the change in Peter's life before he received the Spirit. From Acts 4:8 – 13, describe Peter's life after he received the Spirit.

If God the Holy Spirit can transform Peter, how does his story help you in praying for your loved one?

HIS NEARNESS BRINGS CLARITY

Clarity to the written Word

Apply John 16:13 to a person's struggle to understand God's Word.

According to Ephesians 1:17 – 19, what can you do to help someone who is struggling to understand God's Word?

Clarity to the living Word

Who is the subject of the Bible, according to Luke 24:26 – 27?

Without the Spirit's clarity, how does the world view Jesus?

What is the Holy Spirit's agenda, according to John 16:14 – 15? If you and I are filled with the Spirit, what should our agenda be?

You may feel lonely but you are not alone. Jesus is near. Right here. With you. Now.

Outcast but Not Forsaken

Have you ever been rejected by those who call themselves by God's name? In what way have you, or your loved one, been an "outcast"? Perhaps through divorce? Or division within your church? Or dissension within your family? Or betrayal by a Christian organization or ministry? When God's people reject us, we feel that God has also rejected us. The feeling of isolation and loneliness can be so severe that it may trigger deep depression and even suicidal thoughts.

Read Genesis 21:1 – 21

GOD CARES ABOUT YOU

Hagar, a servant to Abraham's wife, Sarah, was rejected by those who called themselves by God's name. When her son, Ishmael, began to persecute Sarah's son, Isaac, Abraham cast Hagar and her son out of his home. But she was not forsaken. God cared about Hagar and came to her in her desert experience.

God cares about your hurt

From Genesis 16:1 – 16 and 21:1 – 16, describe Hagar.

How was Hagar's attitude in the home reflected in her son? Compare Genesis 16:1 – 4 with 21:9 and Galatians 4:29.

How was Hagar's hurt her own fault? How was it also the fault of others?

Describe as many modern-day parallels to Hagar and her circumstances as you can. For example: She was the second wife of a successful man.

God cares about your helplessness

From Genesis 21:14, describe how Hagar must have felt. Keep in mind that she had been a servant in Abraham's household for twenty-five years.

When have you been treated badly by those who call themselves by God's name? How did you feel?

As someone who suddenly found herself as a single parent, describe some of the challenges Hagar faced.

God cares about your hopelessness

From Genesis 21:15 – 16, what are some of the reasons for Hagar's hopelessness? Apply these reasons for hopelessness to circumstances today.

What caused Hagar to reach the breaking point?

What encouragement from Psalm 72:12 – 13 could you give to someone who is feeling desperately hopeless for some of the same reasons?

What one condition for claiming God's promises in Psalm 72 did Hagar meet? Have you met that same condition?

If God cared enough about an Egyptian servant girl to comfort her after she was cast out, what makes you think He doesn't care about you?

GOD COMES WITH THE HEALING OF HIS PRESENCE

According to Genesis 21:17, why did God intervene?

When have you been blessed by the prayer of your own or someone else's child?

What hurting person are you praying for?

If God knew of Hagar's circumstances, why do you think He questioned Hagar? Compare Genesis 21:12 – 13 with verse 17.

What were some of Hagar's fears? How are they similar to your fears?

GOD COMES WITH THE HEALING OF HIS PROVISION

How did God provide for Hagar's needs in Genesis 21:19?

According to Matthew 6:25 – 26, how will God provide for your needs?

Have you met the same requirement for receiving God's provision that Hagar did? Describe when and how you did.

Apply Psalm 147:3 to the story of Hagar — and to your own story. How does God bind up our wounds? How have you experienced this yourself?

GOD COMES WITH THE HEALING OF HIS PROMISE

From Genesis 21:18, what was God's promise to Hagar? How was the promise fulfilled then? How is it still being fulfilled today?

From the following verses, give phrases that underscore God's faithfulness to keep His promises: Genesis 35:3; 50:24 with Exodus 12:51; Daniel 9:4; Joshua 21:45; 23:14; 2 Chronicles 6:4, 15; Jeremiah 1:12; Ezekiel 12:28; Matthew 5:18.

What comfort for yourself or your loved one do you receive from each of the following promises: Psalm 27:10; 118:6 – 7; Isaiah 43:1 – 2; 65:24, Jeremiah 29:10 – 13; Matthew 6:25 – 33; Romans 8:31; Philippians 4:19; Hebrews 13:5 – 6?

Although Hagar and her son Ishmael were cast out of Abraham's home, they were not forsaken by God. If God cared enough to come to them in the desert, why do you think He will not also come to you in your loneliness and depression?

Bow your head and close your eyes and hear God saying to you, "What is the matter? Do not be afraid. I have heard your cry."

Your Welcome Home!

Have you ever felt unwelcome? Being excluded is a miserable feeling for anyone. And it was a miserable feeling years ago for Geoffrey, a young boy living in the slums of London.

When Geoffrey heard that evangelist D. L. Moody had come to preach in a local church, he decided to go to hear him. After walking all day, Geoffrey arrived at the church as the sun was setting. Just as he was about to enter, a doorman spun him around and asked, "Just where do you think you're going, laddie?" Geoffrey explained that he had walked all the way across London to hear Moody. The doorman looked down at the little boy with uncombed hair, unwashed face, unclean clothes, and unshod feet, then said, "Not you! You're too dirty to go inside!" He folded his arms and stood in front of the door, blocking the entrance.

Geoffrey tried to find another entrance, but all the other doors were locked. Finally, he plopped down on the front steps. Tears began to trickle down his cheeks.

Just then a distinguished-looking gentleman arrived. Noticing the tear stains on the young boy's cheeks, he stopped and asked, "What's wrong?"

Geoffrey blurted out, "I came to hear Dr. Moody preach, but they say I'm too dirty to go inside."

"Here, take my hand," the man said.

Geoffrey placed his grimy little hand in the hand of the stranger, who clasped it tightly and said, "Come with me."

Hand in hand they walked up the steps. The doorkeeper who had forbidden the boy to enter now hastily opened the door wide. With the man still gripping his hand, Geoffrey walked down the center aisle of the church. The man seated him in the front row, then walked to the pulpit and began to preach. The man was D. L. Moody!

Geoffrey was allowed inside the church only because he was holding the hand of D. L. Moody. His acceptance was based solely on his identification and relationship with the great preacher.[1]

After the journey of life, we will look up and see heaven. We're going to long for home, but we are forbidden to enter. Heaven is closed to us because we are too dirty in our sin to enter.

But Jesus offered us His hand at the cross. When we put our hand of faith in His, our sins are forgiven; we enter into a personal relationship with Him and He walks with us hand in hand. And when we reach the gates of heaven, they will be opened wide. Because of our relationship and identification with Him, we will be welcomed into our heavenly home!

Read John 19:38 – 20:18 and Matthew 27:62 – 28:6

WELCOMED BECAUSE HE AROSE — John 19:38 – 20:9

The burial on Friday

Using the following Scriptures, describe the two men who buried Jesus: John 3:1 – 21; 7:40 – 52; Matthew 27:57; Mark 15:43; Luke 23:51.

Why do you think they identified with Jesus in His death when they had been afraid to during His life?

What fear has kept you silent when you should have spoken up for Jesus?

---

1. This true story was told to my mother by Geoffrey (name was changed) when he was an old man.

How do you think the disciples felt when they went to bed on that Friday night?

What is the "Friday" night of your life?

The barriers on Saturday — Matt. 27:62 – 66

According to Matthew 27:62 – 66, what did the religious leaders remember that Jesus' disciples forgot?

What two barriers did the religious leaders erect to make sure no one got into the tomb of Jesus — and no one got out?

What efforts to keep Jesus "buried" are you aware of today?

How do you think the disciples felt on the Saturday following the death and burial of Jesus?

What is the "Saturday" in your life?

The breakout on Sunday — Matt. 28:1 – 6

How effective were the barriers in keeping Jesus buried? See Matthew 28:1 – 6.

When the angel rolled away the stone from the tomb's entrance, did Jesus walk out? If not, how and when did He get out? Relate this to Ephesians 1:18 – 21.

Describe the various reactions to the resurrection of Jesus from Matthew 28:8, 11 – 15, 17; Mark 16:6 – 8; Luke 24:31 – 32, 36 – 45; John 20:20, 24 – 29.

What is the "Sunday" in your life, and how have you responded to it?

How is your faith strengthened by knowing that God raised Jesus from the dead? What "impossible" things are you more able to trust Him with?

WELCOMED BECAUSE HE'S ALIVE — John 20:1 – 18

The spiritual emptiness

From Mark 16:9, what do you think Mary Magdalene's life was like before she met Jesus?

From Matthew 27:55 – 56, what do you think Mary's life was like after she met Jesus?

From Matthew 27:55 – 61, describe Mary's experience on Friday.

How do you think she felt on Saturday?

Give the phrases from Matthew 28:1 – 2, 10 – 11 that reveal Mary's desperation as well as her confusion on Sunday morning.

Without the resurrection, what would be our spiritual state? See 1 Corinthians 15:12 – 19.

The physical evidence

Give the physical evidence for the resurrection of Jesus Christ from each of the following references: Matthew 28:8 – 9, 11 – 15; Luke 24:13 – 35, 39 – 43; John 20:6 – 20, 26 – 28; Acts 4:20; 7:56; 9:1 – 6; 1 Corinthians 15:6.

What evidence is there today for the fact that Jesus is alive?

The personal encounter

What did the angels ask Mary in John 20:13? In what way are people "crying" today?

Put Mary's answer in John 20:13 into your own words.

What did Jesus ask Mary in verse 15? Give examples of people today who are looking for Jesus.

What was Mary's twofold response to her encounter with Jesus? See verses 15 – 18. How was her response similar to those in Acts 4:8 – 13, 18 – 20 and Luke 24:13 – 25?

Why do you think Mary did not recognize Jesus? How could you and I be blinded in the same way to His presence in our lives?

What caused Mary to recognize Jesus was in her life? Link this to John 10:3 – 4, 14; Romans 10:17.

Mary's day, which had begun with such heartache and emptiness, ended with joy when Jesus told her, "I am returning to my Father and your Father, to my God and your God" (John 20:17). In other words, because of His death and resurrection, now His God is ours, His Father is ours, and His heavenly home is ours as well. Jesus was announcing the good news that sinners who have been cleansed by His blood and saved by His grace are now born again into His family and will one day be welcomed into His heavenly home! Now that is a message to tell!

March

HARDSHIP

Five Things a Storm Can't Destroy

Hurricane season is a terrifying time for those in locations that bear the brunt of the storms' wrath. The eastern part of the United States has often been hit with one deadly, destructive storm after another. We grieve with those who have lost loved ones and weep with those who have lost businesses, homes, cars, and keepsakes. Our minds reel at the overwhelming task of cleaning up. We know that millions of lives will never be the same.

While the newspapers are filled with news of the storms' terror, many people across our nation and the world are experiencing storms that are just as devastating, yet not as obvious: storms of divorce, disease, or death; storms of betrayal, bankruptcy, or blindness; storms of abuse, adultery, or addiction; storms that leave shattered lives, broken hearts, and shredded hopes; storms that turn dreams into nightmares.

My home and extended family have not been exempt from storms. We have been affected by all of the hurricanes to some degree — and we have been hit by the less-visible storms as well. As I have cried out to God for help, He has reminded me of five things that I have in the midst of any storm — five things that never can be destroyed by wind, flood, fire, terrorism, enemy attack, or anything else.

What storm has struck your life? If you are God's child through faith in Jesus Christ, He also promises the same five things to you.

YOU HAVE HIS PURPOSE

Give a phrase from Mark 6:45 that shows that the disciples were in God's will when the storm struck.

From the following verses, list other storms that swept across the lives of those Jesus loved, who also were in God's will: John 11:1 – 3; Acts 4:1 – 3; 7:55 – 60; 14:19 – 20; 16:22 – 24; 27:1 – 44; Revelation 1:9.

Because storms come into the lives of everyone, what unique promise is given to those who belong to God by faith in Jesus Christ when they experience storms? See Romans 8:28.

Would you ask God to give you a glimpse of the purpose for which He has allowed a storm to sweep through your life?

YOU HAVE HIS PRAYERS

What do you think Jesus was praying about in Mark 6:46? See John 6:14 – 15 for help with your answer.

How is this same attitude a concern for prayer today?

For whom do you think Jesus was praying?

Give phrases from John 17 that reveal how Jesus prays for you and me, especially when we are in the midst of a storm.

What does Hebrews 7:25 say about His prayers for you?

Put into your own words what it means to you to know that Jesus is praying for you, now, while you are in the midst of your storm. Thank Jesus now for praying for you.

YOU HAVE HIS PRESENCE

After prayer, what did Jesus do?

Give phrases that reveal Jesus is not indifferent to our storms. See Mark 6:47 – 48; John 9:1, 35; 11:33 – 35. How do you think He feels about your personal storms?

Which of the following promises is most encouraging to you, and why? See Exodus 33:14; Joshua 1:9; 2 Chronicles 20:15, 17; Psalm 23:4; Isaiah 43:1 – 2; Matthew 28:20; Hebrews 13:5.

Spend a few moments in quiet reflection on these promises until deep within your spirit you are reassured of His presence with you.

What did the disciples have to do before they could experience Jesus' peace? See Mark 6:48 – 50; John 6:21.

Why do you think Jesus almost passed by in Mark 6:48? Relate this to Ezekiel 36:37 (KJV) and John 14:13 – 14.

What do you have to do to experience His presence and His peace in the midst of your storm? Compare Hosea 7:14 with Psalm 18:3 – 19.

Have you called out to the Lord? If not, what are you waiting for?

What do the following verses tell us about peace in the midst of the storm? See Luke 24:36 – 39; John 14:27; 16:33; 20:19 – 20; Ephesians 2:14; Philippians 4:6 – 7.

Describe an experience of supernatural peace in the midst of a storm in your life.

YOU HAVE HIS POWER

From the following verses, how was the power of Christ revealed on the lake in Mark 6:51 and in Luke 8:23 – 25? On the mountain in Mark 9:2 – 7? In the valley in Mark 9:14 – 27? On land in John 9:1 – 7? At the tomb in John 11:38 – 44? At the end of human history in Revelation 19:11 – 21?

Is this same power available to you and me today? See Acts 1:8; 2 Corinthians 12:9; 2 Timothy 1:7.

Pray Paul's prayer in Ephesians 1:18 – 21 for yourself.

Storms can be sudden and fierce, raging until they suck the life out of us. When the storm comes — as it did in Isaiah's life in the year that King Uzziah died (Isaiah 6:1 – 5) — don't look back or around or ahead. Look up and ask God to give you a fresh vision of His purpose, His prayers, His presence, His peace, and His power. Then reach out to comfort someone else by just giving them Jesus!

King David faced many perilous times, including personal attacks, enemy invasions, national war, and family betrayal. He understood the feeling of fear, yet responded with confidence. Psalm 27 is a prayer that reveals his attitude in the face of war. There are many different types of wars: wars between nations, wars within the heart, wars within the home, wars on our streets, and wars in our culture. Life is not easy. We often cannot choose our circumstances, but we can choose how we respond to them.

Read Psalm 27

CONFIDENT IN GOD'S PERSON — Ps. 27:1 – 3

List the four situations that could have caused David great fear. See Psalm 27:1 – 3. Apply each one to a contemporary situation or an experience in your own life.

How did David describe God? Why do you think that these particular characteristics were an antidote to his fears?

What two deliberate choices did David make? How could he make these choices? On what was his confidence based?

When Joshua faced war, how did God challenge him to make similar choices in Joshua 1:9? What about Jehoshaphat in 2 Chronicles 20:15, 17? The children of Israel in Deuteronomy 20:1, 3 – 4?

How did Habakkuk make a similar choice in Habakkuk 3:16 – 19?

What is hindering you from making the same kinds of choices?

CONFIDENT IN GOD'S PROTECTION — Ps 27:4

According to Psalm 27:4, what was the priority of David's life?

What do you think "the house of the Lord" represents? See Psalm 91:1 – 2.

Describe the Lord's "beauty" from the following verses: Psalm 34:8; Nahum 1:7; Ephesians 2:7; Deuteronomy 3:24; Isaiah 6:3; Ephesians 2:4 – 5; 1 John 4:16; Job 37:22; 1 Chronicles 29:12; 2 Chronicles 25:8; Psalm 62:11 – 12; 119:137; Daniel 2:20; John 1:18; Hebrews 1:1 – 3; Colossians 1:15 – 20.

When you reflect on God's beauty or character as you face conflict, what comfort do you receive from Isaiah 43:1 – 2; Psalm 46:1 – 11; 91:1 – 16?

Name at least five of David's requests as he poured out his heart to God in prayer. See Psalm 27:5 – 12. Give a practical application for each request.

What are you asking God to do for you? When do you pray? Are you praying more this week than you did last week? Write your own requests of God.

In Psalm 27:9, what name does David give to God? How does this name encourage your confidence?

Read the following verses, and list phrases that encourage you: Psalm 72:13; Isaiah 63:9; Romans 8:31 – 39; Titus 3:4 – 5.

In spite of the turmoil around him, on what did David focus in Psalm 27:11?

Where is your focus in troubled times? When do you read your Bible? Are you reading it more this week than you did last week?

CONFIDENT IN GOD'S PURPOSE — Ps. 27:13 – 14

What phrase in Psalm 27:13 – 14 indicates that God did not deliver David immediately? How does this passage compare to Psalm 23; Isaiah 40:27 – 31; Lamentations 3:19 – 26?

What enabled David to overcome his fears in the end? How do you and I overcome our fears? See Hebrews 11:32 – 34; 1 John 5:4.

How was David's faith strengthened by his experiences? See 1 Samuel 17:34 – 37, 45 – 50.

Do you think your confidence in God is strengthened more in times of comfort or in times of crisis? Could this be one of God's purposes in allowing us to face war and conflict?

As you face trouble within and without, trust God. Just trust Him. Trust Him now!

Have you ever wondered if you could maintain your commitment to Christ under intense pressure and persecution?

Have you ever wondered what happened to the disciples of Jesus? According to tradition:

- Philip was scourged and crucified.
- Matthew was nailed to the ground with spikes and beheaded.
- Jude was beaten to death with sticks and clubs.
- Simon was tortured and crucified.
- John, son of Zebedee, was tortured and exiled.
- James, brother of John, was beheaded.
- James was pushed from the top of a building; then his broken body was beaten to death.
- Andrew, Peter's brother, hung on a cross for three days before dying.
- Bartholomew was beaten and skinned alive before being beheaded.
- Thomas was speared with a javelin.
- And Peter was crucified — upside down.

Every single one of our Lord's beloved disciples suffered cruel torture. Why? Not for saying Jesus of Nazareth had been crucified — the world knew of and confirmed His death. The disciples were tortured, vilified, exiled, and executed for saying He had risen from the dead. They were put to death for their conviction that Jesus Christ is alive and that He is Lord!

Have you ever wondered if you could maintain your commitment to Christ under intense pressure and persecution?

How can you and I be faithful to the end?

The apostle Peter penned a letter to the early church that exuded passionate love for Christ and exuberant joy in knowing Him, even though his relationship with Christ would cost him his life within the year. How could he maintain a joyous, faithful commitment to the end?

Peter kept looking up.

Read 1 Peter 1:1 – 12

FOCUSED ON GOD'S GRACE

Chosen by the Father — 1 Peter 1:1 – 2a

Describe Peter's initial encounter with Jesus in Luke 5:1 – 11. Give the phrase that reveals Peter's commitment to Christ from the beginning.

How does John 15:16, 19 confirm 1 Peter 1:2?

Describe your initial encounter with Jesus. What has been your commitment to Him since that moment?

Read Ephesians 1:3 – 6. With what spiritual blessings has God blessed you? According to these verses, why has He blessed you?

Changed by the Spirit — 1 Peter 1:2b

From the following verses, describe areas of Peter's life that needed to be changed: Mark 8:31 – 33; 9:2 – 7; 14:32 – 42; John 18:1 – 11; Matthew 26:31 – 35, 69 – 75.

Who would change Peter and how? See Acts 1:8; 2:14 – 18, 32 – 33; 4:8; 2 Corinthians 3:18.

What changes can be seen in your life as a result of your salvation?

How are you encouraged by 1 Peter 1:2; 2 Thessalonians 2:13?

Cleansed by the Son — 1 Peter 1:2c

What was Peter's original reaction when Jesus told him of the cross? See Mark 8:32.

How does Acts 4:8 – 12 reveal that Peter changed his mind about the cross?

What did the blood and death of Jesus do for Peter — and for you? Give phrases from the following verses: Ephesians 1:7; Hebrews 10:19 – 22; 1 John 1:7; Revelation 7:13 – 14; 12:11.

Living hope — 1 Peter 1:3

Keeping in mind that the last words Jesus heard Peter say before the cross were words of denial, what do you think the following meant to Peter: Luke 24:12; Mark 16:7; Luke 24:33 – 34; John 21:1 – 22?

Describe a time when God has given you another chance.

How does Peter's experience give credibility to his words in 1 Peter 1:6 – 7?

God brought blessing and glory from the horror of the cross. What good might He bring from your present suffering?

Lasting inheritance — 1 Peter 1:4 – 5

How does Ephesians 1:3 – 5 describe our "lasting inheritance"?

How is this confirmed by John 1:16?

Make an alphabetized list of some of the blessings that are yours through faith in Christ. Memorize it so that you can repeat it to yourself and cultivate an "attitude of gratitude."

As Peter stared death in the face, why would this inheritance be especially meaningful?

Describe God's glory from the following verses: Exodus 16:10; 24:17; 34:29; 2 Chronicles 7:1 – 3; John 1:14; 2 Corinthians 4:6.

Give the phrases from 1 Peter 1:6 – 9 that indicate Peter's focus remained on the glory of God in the face of Jesus Christ.

What are some practical things you can do to keep your focus on Christ?

Their promise — 1 Peter 1:10 – 11

From the following verses, describe the promise of the gospel God gave to His people even though they did not know the details of it: Genesis 3:15 with 3:23. And Genesis 12:3 with Galatians 3:16; Deuteronomy 18:18; Isaiah 9:6 – 7; 53:1 – 5.

How does Hebrews 11:39 – 40 speak to this?

Our possession — 1 Peter 1:12

How does a person "possess" the gospel? See Ephesians 1:13.

How did you first hear the gospel? Who "preached the gospel to you by the Holy Spirit" (1 Peter 1:12)?

When did the promise of the gospel become your possession?

What are you doing and what will you do to share the gospel with others?

Living in a world that is shaken by tsunamis, typhoons, and terrorism; mudslides, snowstorms, and suicide bombers; disease, destruction, and death; floods, famine, and fear — you can face tomorrow because He lives. Stay focused on Him — and keep looking up!

I Needed That Storm

Have you ever watched a storm brewing? Because of the wide-open spaces at the beach, my family and I were once able to sit out on a deck and watch a summer storm taking shape on the horizon. We could hear the rumble of thunder as the purple-black clouds piled higher into the sky, and we could see the pulsating glow as lightning flashed in the distance. As we dashed for safety, the storm broke all around us with deafening ferocity. Then it passed, exiting in a glorious sunset, leaving the ocean sparkling and the earth refreshed.

As I watch the evening news on television and read the morning paper, I feel like I'm watching a storm build on the horizon of the world. It seems only a matter of time before it breaks out all around us. I hope by the time you read this, the clouds will have broken and brilliant sunshine will have prevailed.

Yet I can't help but wonder, is there a storm building in your life? A storm of ill health? Job loss? A broken relationship? Death? As terrifying as storms can be and as much damage as they can do, sometimes I find that I actually need a storm.

Read Nahum 1:3 and Daniel 3

TO OPEN MY EYES TO HIS PRESENCE

How does Nahum 1:3 describe God's presence in the midst of the storm?

How does Luke 9:34 – 36 seem to confirm that God can be in the "clouds"?

Read Ezekiel 1:1 – 5, 22, 26 – 28. When and how did God reveal His presence to Ezekiel?

Read Isaiah 6:1. What major event in Judah's history did God use to open Isaiah's eyes? What has God done to open your eyes?

Describe the experience the three Hebrew children had in Daniel 3:8 – 27; the experience the disciples had in Mark 6:45 – 51; the experience John had in Revelation 1:9 – 17.

Could God be trying to reveal Himself to you in the clouds of your life? How?

TO BEND MY KNEES IN PRAYER

Read Psalm 50:3 – 15. Divide the verses into phrases that address the presence of God, prayer, power, and praise.

What helps motivate us to pray? Give phrases from Psalm 50:15; 86:6 – 7; James 5:13.

Why do you think troubles, or "storms," compel us to pray?

Describe the storms that compelled prayer in the following passages and apply each to life today: Genesis 18:20 – 33; Joshua 7:1 – 9; 1 Samuel 1:1 – 20; 2 Chronicles 18:3 – 4; 20:1 – 6; Daniel 9:1 – 4; Ezra 9:1 – 6; Nehemiah 1:1 – 11; Mark 14:27 – 36; Acts 4:1 – 31.

Which of these storms have you experienced? How did the storm affect your prayer life?

TO LIVE MY LIFE WITH POWER

What do you think is required in order to experience God's power? Read Matthew 8:5 – 13; 20:29 – 34; John 9:1 – 7; Acts 1:8.

How did the people in each of the following passages experience God's power? How was that experience related to prayer? Read Exodus 14:5 – 31; 1 Kings 18:16 – 39; John 11:38 – 44; Acts 12:1 – 17; 16:16 – 34.

When have you truly experienced God's power? On reflection, was there a link between your experience of His power and prayer — either your own prayer or someone else's?

TO FILL MY LIPS WITH PRAISE

From the following passages, describe the journey that led to praise: Exodus 15:1 – 18; 2 Samuel 22:1 – 7; Jeremiah 3:19 – 23; Psalm 13:1 – 6; 34:1 – 10; Daniel 2:1 – 23; Habakkuk 3:16 – 19. How does praise help us along the journey, especially when we encounter storms? See Isaiah 61:3.

Read Psalm 27:1 – 6. Which phrases refer to God's presence? Prayer? Power? Praise?

Do you think your praise would be as full and heartfelt if you had never experienced God's presence, God's answers to prayer, and God's power — especially during a storm? Could that be one reason God has allowed the clouds to gather on the horizon of your life?

If an eagle wants to soar in the sky, it needs a storm to provide wind currents to lift it into heights it could not otherwise achieve on its own. If you want to soar higher in your personal experience with God, do you need a storm too? Name your storm. Thank God for how He can use it in your life. Then spread your wings of faith and get ready to soar.

Our Refuge from the Storm

One afternoon as I sat in a little mountain cabin, preparing for my annual seminar at The Cove, I became aware that it was growing dark outside. The wind picked up, bending the trees double as it roared along the ridge like a jet plane terribly off course. Tree branches snapped under the strain, sounding as though some phantom hunter with a shotgun was recklessly opening fire. I looked out the window and saw a gray curtain sweeping across the little valley, and I knew the rain was coming. It did! Within moments, the cabin was under a deluge that could be likened to perpendicular white water rapids.

As the storm unleashed all of its fury outside the cabin, inside I was snuggled under a blanket, curled up in an easy chair beside a crackling fire, with a cup of hot coffee in my hand and an open Bible on my lap. And I thanked God for a safe, dry, comfortable refuge from the storm.

Then I thought of the storms that raged in my life. And I quietly bowed my head and thanked God again for His refuge from the storms …

Read Isaiah 43:1 – 7

What storm is raging on the outside of you?

Has war invaded your family? Have you been diagnosed with a dreaded disease? Are you facing death … or the death of a loved one?

God is our help in danger

In each of the following passages, give the word or phrase that describes our refuge from the storm of danger: Psalm 27:1 – 3, 5; 46:1 – 11; Romans 8:31 – 39. How does each phrase encourage you? How could you use it to encourage someone else?

Describe the danger to God's people in 2 Kings 6:8 – 23. What phrase in this passage encourages you when you feel surrounded by the enemy? Relate it to Psalm 34:7; 1 John 4:4.

What is God's promise to us when we are facing danger? See Isaiah 43:1 – 2.

Describe how God's people experienced the refuge of His help in danger: Moses in Exodus 14:5 – 14, 21 – 31; David in 1 Samuel 17:34 – 37, 41 – 50; Jehoshaphat in 2 Chronicles 20:1 – 4, 14 – 22; three Hebrew slaves in Daniel 3:1 – 27; Daniel in Daniel 6:1 – 28; Peter in Acts 12:1 – 11.

How have you experienced God's help in danger?

God is our healer in disease

What disease has afflicted you or your loved one?

Pray over the following promises and ask God to give you one to claim. See Exodus 15:26; 23:25; Psalm 41:3; 103:1 – 4; Matthew 8:14 – 17.

Is it possible that Jesus had passed by and chosen not to heal the crippled man in Acts 3:1 – 10? Did Jesus heal everybody? Give a phrase from Mark 1:34; 3:10; Luke 4:24 – 27 that indicates He did not.

How does Jesus teach us in John 11:1 – 41 that if He does not heal us, it's because He has a greater purpose? What is it?

How did the apostle Paul experience a "greater purpose" than physical healing? See 2 Corinthians 12:7 – 10.

If you need the refuge of His healing, how do John 14:13 – 14 and Matthew 26:39 help you to pray?

God is our hope in death

How does a child of God face death differently than a nonbeliever? See 1 Thessalonians 4:13.

From the following verses, give aspects of our refuge of hope in death: Job 19:25 – 27; Psalm 23:4, 6; John 14:1 – 3; 2 Corinthians 5:6 – 8; 1 Corinthians 15:42 – 44, 53 – 57.

STORMS WITHIN

Sometimes the storms on the outside of us are nothing compared with the storms that rage within us. What storm has unleashed its fury within you?

God is our provision in want

What physical, emotional, and material needs do you have that are not being met?

What encouragement do you receive from each of the following verses: Isaiah 43:18 – 21; 58:11; 61:1 – 3; Philippians 4:19?

What "mount" is the place where all of our needs are met ultimately? Compare Genesis 22:14 with Luke 23:33.

God is our peace in worry

What are you worried about?

Does worrying help you or the situation you're worried about? See Matthew 7:27.

When tempted to worry, what are you to do? Give one action item from each of the following verses: Matthew 6:25 – 26, 32 – 33; Mark 13:11; Philippians 4:6 – 7; Proverbs 3:5 – 6.

God is our power in weakness

What weakness are you struggling to overcome?

Why do you think God allows us to be weak? See 1 Corinthians 1:26 – 29; 2 Corinthians 4:7 – 10.

Why doesn't God accept weakness as an excuse for our lack of victory over temptation as well as our lack of commitment to live for and serve Him? See Philippians 4:13; Ephesians 1:18 – 20.

On the day when we gather around God's throne and sing praises to the Lamb, what testimony of His power will be on your lips? See Revelation 5:13.

Take a moment now and thank God for being your refuge from the storms.

April

GRACE

As we prepare to celebrate Easter, stop and think what it would have been like to live before Christ died on the cross. What would it be like to have a heart cry to know God and to live in His presence, yet be separated from Him by the formality of religion or the rigidity of the law? What would it be like to follow God's prescribed way of reconciliation through a blood sacrifice, only to walk away from it knowing your sins were not really forgiven — nor were you any closer to the most holy place of God's presence than you were before the sacrifice?

The writer to the Hebrews reveals that the hope of the cross was always before people in the Old Testament, but only in sacrifices, symbols, and shadows.

Read Hebrews 10:1 – 25

IN THE SACRIFICES

Sacrifices that were not perfect

Were the Old Testament sacrifices effective in taking away sin? Give phrases from the following verses to support your answer: Hebrews 7:27; 9:7 – 9; 10:1.

If the sacrifices were ineffective in reconciling man to God, why were they made? See Hebrews 9:7 – 10, 20 – 22; 10:3, 8.

What has the cross (new covenant) done for us that the Old Testament system of sacrifices could not? See Hebrews 7:23 – 25, 27; 8:8 – 12; 9:12 – 14, 15, 26 – 28; 10:10, 15 – 17.

Can you add to Jesus' sacrifice to make it more effective from God's perspective? Write out Hebrews 10:14 in your own words.

What have you been trying to add to the cross — perhaps subconsciously — to make it more effective? Religion? Rituals? Traditions? Good works? _____? Fill in the blank.

Celebrate Easter by thanking God that Christ's death is perfect and complete in itself and by placing your faith in Jesus Christ alone for forgiveness of sin and reconciliation with God.

Sacrifices that were not pleasing

Generally speaking, was God pleased with the Old Testament sacrifices? See Hebrews 10:5 – 6.

If He was not pleased, why wasn't He? See Hebrews 8:8 – 9; 9:10, 13.

What are some of the reasons that God is pleased with the sacrifice of Jesus Christ? See Hebrews 7:22 – 28; 9:14; 10:8 – 14.

How does Hebrews 10:5 – 10 answer those who say there are ways to God other than through the cross of Christ?

What other punishment (besides the cross) do people today believe that God inflicts for the condemnation of sin? What verses could you use to reassure them that God is totally pleased with the cross?

Celebrate Easter by thanking God that Christ's death on the cross is completely pleasing to Him. Don't try to make it more pleasing by adding to it.

Sacrifices that were not powerful

Taking into account the thousands of sacrifices made in Old Testament times during the course of a person's life — and the rivers of blood that were shed — what difference did the sacrifices make? See Hebrews 5:1 – 3.

If another way to think of being made holy is to be made whole, what astounding revelation does Hebrews 10:10 give us?

Consider the verb tense used in Hebrews 10:10. What does this mean to you?

In what way are you seeking to remove memories of sin? Of a sinful stronghold? Of sinful habits? Of sinful attitudes?

From the following Scriptures, give phrases that apply to this purifying, powerful impact of the cross: Isaiah 53:4 – 6; 1 Corinthians 1:17 – 18; Ephesians 1:7; Colossians 1:20; 2:13 – 15; 1 John 1:7 – 9; Revelation 1:5.

Celebrate Easter by confessing all known sin in your life and asking God to cleanse you. Thank Him that the cross has not lost its power to change lives, and ask God to change yours!

IN THE SYMBOLS

Relate the symbolic, prophetic promise of Genesis 3:15 to the cross, keeping in mind that the serpent is the Devil and the seed of the woman is Jesus.

In what way do you see the cross in the symbolism of Numbers 21:4 – 9? Compare it with John 3:14; John 6:40.

Celebrate Easter by telling someone else that the cross is not a symbol of something to come, but a testimony to what has already been done.

IN THE SHADOWS

From the following verses, give one word that specifically indicates how long the cross is effective: Hebrews 10:14; John 3:16; Romans 6:22.

Read Hebrews 10:14. Can you lose your forgiveness, salvation, or eternal life? How does that affect your faith?

From Hebrews 10:19 – 22, what has been opened up exclusively for us because of the cross? See Romans 5:9 – 11.

From Hebrews 10:22 – 25, if you have been to the cross for forgiveness of sin, what are five things you are challenged to do? Write each one and how it applies to your life. Be specific and practical.

Celebrate Easter by implementing each of these five things with a heart full of gratitude that we live on this side of the cross.

Praise God that we no longer live in the shadows, content with symbols and insufficient sacrifices. Praise God that we live on this side of the cross. Praise God for Jesus!

It's Time for Good News

Every day we are bombarded with bad news: children are abducted; natural disasters devastate lives all over the world; people kill strangers and loved ones; people we have looked up to fail ... the list goes on. It seems endless.

Early in the first century, Judah lived under Roman occupation. The narrow city streets of Jerusalem echoed with the sound of marching Roman soldiers, and the hillsides were dotted with victims hanging on crosses. Surely, people then too were weighed down by bad things. Many people had incurable diseases; the religious system was corrupted by priests appointed by the Roman oppressors; taxes collected for Rome had almost reached extortion levels. And God seemed silent.

Then one day, in a small synagogue of Nazareth, the son of a local carpenter's widow stood and read from the prophet Isaiah. When He sat down, He announced that Isaiah's words were fulfilled in Him that very day. He had come to proclaim good news!

Read Luke 4:18 – 19

THE GOOD NEWS OF FORGIVENESS OF SIN

"He has anointed me to preach good news to the poor" (Luke 4:18a).

According to Matthew 5:3; Revelation 3:14 – 17; and 2 Corinthians 8:9, who are the poor?

Why do we need forgiveness? See Genesis 2:16 – 17; 3:6 – 19; 1 Corinthians 15:21 – 22; Romans 3:23; 6:23.

What was the price God paid to offer us forgiveness of sin? Give phrases from the following: Hebrews 9:22; Ephesians 1:7; Acts 4:11 – 12; 1 Peter 1:18 – 19.

How do we obtain forgiveness from God for our sin? See John 3:16; 14:6; 1 John 2:2.

Write the unique aspect of the good news that is announced in each of the following verses: Romans 5:6 – 8; John 1:12; 3:16 – 18; 14:1 – 3; Romans 6:23; Hebrews 7:25; 10:17; 13:5; Galatians 3:26 – 28; Ephesians 1:13 – 14; Revelation 21:3 – 4.

Look at Acts 2:21; 2 Peter 3:9; 1 Timothy 2:3 – 6. To whom does God make His offer of salvation?

Describe in your own words the first time you heard the good news of forgiveness of sin. Who announced the good news to you? When did you accept God's offer of forgiveness?

"He has sent me to proclaim freedom for the prisoners and recovery of sight for the blind, to release the oppressed" (Luke 4:18b).

From the following verses, explain how someone can see, yet be blind: John 9:39 – 41; Matthew 7:3 – 5; 2 Peter 1:5 – 9; James 1:22 – 25; Revelation 3:15 – 17.

What are some specific things that oppress people or hold them captive? Consider Romans 6:12, 16; 7:22 – 24; Hebrews 2:14 – 15.

Do you know a "prisoner"? Pray for that person now.

What things hold you captive, hindering you from freely living for Christ? Is your freedom in Christ worth trading for any one of them?

Give phrases from the following verses that encourage those who are oppressed: Matthew 11:28 – 30; Hosea 11:4; Nahum 1:13; Zephaniah 3:17 – 20; Matthew 1:21; John 10:10; 1 Corinthians 1:21; Hebrews 9:15; Romans 8:1.

Which of these verses will you share this week with someone you know who is blind, oppressed, or held captive?

THE GOOD NEWS OF FAVOR WITH GOD

"To proclaim the year of the Lord's favor" (Luke 4:19).

Favor nationally

Using Deuteronomy 28:1 – 14 as a guide, make a comprehensive list of all the blessings God has poured out on our country.

What are some of the warnings that God gave ancient Israel in Deuteronomy 28:15 – 58 that any country would do well to heed? Name some of the consequences already happening in our own country that you think may be a result of not heeding the warnings.

If any nation is sliding into judgment and losing God's favor, what should she do, according to 2 Chronicles 7:13 – 14?

What encourages you in 2 Chronicles 7:15?

How were these promises claimed by Daniel, then fulfilled by God? See Daniel 9:1 – 6, 17 – 19; Ezra 1:1 – 4.

If God blessed Judah when Daniel cried out to Him on her behalf, do you think this could be the year of God's blessing — if those called by His name would pray?

Favor personally

What are some of the conditions that Israel needed to meet in order to receive the Lord's blessings, according to Deuteronomy 6:5 – 9, 18, 24 – 25; 7:9 – 15?

Although we are saved through grace and not by obeying the law (Romans 8:3 – 4), what do you need to do in a practical way to live in accordance with God's standards as seen in the above passages?

What two conditions need to be met in order to receive all of God's spiritual blessings, as described in Ephesians 1:4? Have you met those conditions?

From Ephesians 1:1 – 23, list at least ten blessings that God offers. Explain what each one means to you.

Consider Romans 11:33 – 36; Ephesians 1:16 – 19; 3:16, 20; Philippians 4:19; John 1:14, 16. What phrases indicate God's supply of blessings that He is able to pour out on all who belong to Him?

In a world of despair and increasing hopelessness, it is important that you and I do not lose our focus. Our focus is not on the despair, misery, and hate — it is not on the problems, crises, or disasters. Our focus is on Jesus and the forgiveness, freedom, and favor that He offers! Saturated in doom and gloom, many people are looking for answers — for something that makes sense of the senseless and gives hope to the hopeless. You and I have the answer — it's Jesus! There has never been a more strategic, opportune time to tell others about Him. Let's proclaim the good news — now!

Who do you think is beyond hope when it comes to salvation? Is there someone you have dropped off your prayer list because that person seems to be beyond the reach of God's grace? Then be encouraged by the personal testimony of one of the most wicked kings in history.

At one time, Nebuchadnezzar was king of the greatest empire in the world (Daniel 2:37 – 38). He was also one of the most evil leaders in human history — the tyrant who threw three Hebrew men into the fiery furnace when they refused to bow to his image (Daniel 3:13 – 23). This same Nebuchadnezzar was converted! He wrote down his testimony as a witness not only to the world of his day but also to future generations.

Read Daniel 4

HE WAS PERSONALLY CHANGED: WHAT GOD DID — Dan. 4:1 – 3

In what way did God change Nebuchadnezzar's priorities? Compare Daniel 3:13 – 15 with 4:1. His preoccupation? Compare 4:30 with 4:2. His perspective? Compare 3:15 with 4:3, 34 – 35.

If there has been no personal change as a result of faith in Jesus Christ, can a person go to heaven? See Matthew 18:3.

What does James say about a professed faith that gives no evidence of change? See James 2:17.

When were you personally changed or converted? What changes has Jesus made in your life that others can see?

HE WAS POWERFULLY CHANGED: HOW GOD DID IT — Dan. 4:4–35

God created a need

Describe the condition of Nebuchadnezzar's life in Daniel 4:4.

What spiritual needs do you think he was aware of? Material needs? Emotional needs? Physical needs?

How did his condition change in verses 5–18?

What needs are you aware of in the life of your "Nebuchadnezzar"?

God clarified His Word

What different emphases did Daniel give in his presentation of God's Word in Daniel 4:19 – 23? 24 – 26? 27? How are these important today?

How necessary is God's Word to change or to conversion? See Romans 10:17; Hebrews 11:6; 1 John 2:3 – 6.

What have you done to make sure your "Nebuchadnezzar" hears the Word of God?

God crushed Nebuchadnezzar's pride

What was Nebuchadnezzar's response to hearing God's Word explained and applied to his life? See Daniel 4:27 – 30.

How long did God wait for Nebuchadnezzar to repent of his sin? See Daniel 4:29.

What evidence is there that God's patience did not mean toleration or acceptance of sin? See Daniel 4:31 – 33.

What are some ways God brings people to repentance? See 2 Chronicles 33:1 – 2, 10 – 13; Jonah 1:4, 17; Acts 9:1 – 9; 16:26 – 30; Romans 2:4.

Whose responsibility is it to convict your "Nebuchadnezzar" of sin? See John 16:7 – 11.

In what way might you be trying to do the Holy Spirit's job? Cease pointing out the sin in that person's life and just pray for your "Nebuchadnezzar."

God changed Nebuchadnezzar's mind

In Daniel 4:34, what was involved when Nebuchadnezzar raised his eyes toward heaven? Compare Daniel 4:25 with verses 34 – 35.

God changed Nebuchadnezzar. Why is it hard to believe He can change the person you are praying for?

How is God working in the life of your "Nebuchadnezzar" to create an awareness of a need for Him? To clarify His Word? To crush pride? To change thinking and bring that person to repentance?

HE WAS PURPOSEFULLY CHANGED: WHY GOD DID IT — Dan. 4:36 – 37

What were the practical results of Nebuchadnezzar's conversion? See Daniel 4:36.

What was the ultimate spiritual and eternal result of his conversion? See Daniel 4:37.

What is the ultimate purpose of your conversion? See Matthew 5:16; Romans 15:5 – 6; 1 Corinthians 6:20.

Take a few minutes now to thank God for what He did for Nebuchadnezzar of old.

Thank God for what He has done for you, how He has done it, and why He has done it.

Make time today to write down your personal testimony as a witness to those who may read it, including future generations of children and grandchildren.

Persevere in prayer for your "Nebuchadnezzar."

Go and Tell

We are blessed to have many wonderful Bible studies in North America. Studies are offered in churches, homes, schools, dorms, apartments, and lunchrooms. There are studies that are video-driven, lesson-driven, discussion-driven, and lecture-driven. There are studies for just about everyone — men, women, teenagers, singles, the elderly, students, businessmen, businesswomen, government leaders, and any combination of the above. Sometimes I wonder: when it comes to the Scripture, have we become more comfortable with thinking and studying than with actually doing what it says?

I have been struck in so many ways by Mary Magdalene's example. She had been a disciple of Jesus from the time He set her free from vicious inner torment. She was at Calvary and watched from a discreet distance as He was crucified. She saw Him die; she saw Him buried. The Sunday morning following the crucifixion, she encountered the risen Christ. In the thrill of the moment, as she flung her arms around Him, she was instructed to stop clinging to Him. Jesus commissioned her to go and tell others of her experience with the risen Lord. Could it be that the risen Lord would tell you and me to stop clinging to Him — to stop spending all of our time reading the Bible and praying and gathering in our little holy huddles? The time has come to go and tell others about Jesus!

Read Matthew 28 and John 20:10 – 18

ACCEPT THE INVITATION

Make sure that your faith is not based on hearsay or on secondhand information, but on your own examination of the evidence and on your own experience with the risen Christ.

What did the angel invite the women to do in Matthew 28:6?

Have you accepted the invitation to examine — for yourself — the facts for the resurrection of Jesus Christ? How have you responded?

List as many facts as you can that give evidence for the bodily resurrection of Jesus Christ. See Matthew 28:1 – 17; Luke 24:13 – 31, 34; John 20:1 – 29; Acts 9:1 – 6; 1 Corinthians 15:6.

What other evidence for the resurrection can you give from Scripture? From history? From today's world?

Describe your own firsthand encounter with the risen Lord Jesus Christ.

OBEY THE COMMAND

Only when you've accepted the good news of Christ's resurrection, and made a commitment to Him, can you truly obey His commands.

What command did the angels give to the women in Matthew 28:7? Write it in your own words.

How many times is the command repeated in Matthew 28? Give the context of each command, applying it to your life.

How did Mary receive and respond to this command in John 20:10 – 16?

Describe the obedience to Jesus' command in each of the following stories: Acts 3:1 – 10; 4:1 – 20, 23 – 31; 5:27 – 42.

In each of these stories, what was the response to the disciples' obedience?

What other command was given to disciples about speaking out for Christ? See 2 Timothy 1:7 – 8; John 14:27; Acts 18:9.

Read Acts 18:9. What does it mean to you that the apostle Paul himself may have been afraid to witness?

What do you not understand about the command to "go and tell"?

CLAIM THE PROMISES

Very often in Scripture, commands are coupled with promises that are conditioned by our obedience to the commands.

The promise of His power

According to Matthew 28:18, describe the scope of Jesus' authority.

Can you think of anything over which He does not have authority? See Ephesians 1:22. What does this mean to you personally?

How does the Holy Spirit change your life? See Acts 1:8.

How does Paul describe this power in Ephesians 1:18 – 21?

How does Paul encourage an apparently timid witness in 2 Timothy 1:7?

If you don't "go and tell" others about Jesus, how will you know for sure that God has given you the power to do so?

The promise of His presence

According to Acts 1:4 – 5, 8, what is the key to being an effective witness for Christ?

What is the seeming contradiction between Acts 1:9 and Matthew 28:20? Explain in your own words why these verses do not contradict each other.

How did God fulfill the promise of His presence in the following passages: Daniel 3; 6; 2 Timothy 4:16 – 18; Revelation 1:9 – 12?

What are some of the situations in which God promises to be with you, according to Joshua 1:9; Psalm 23:4; 139:18; Isaiah 41:9 – 10; 43:2; Amos 5:14; John 14:1 – 3?

Read Matthew 28:18 – 20

If you have personally accepted the invitation to encounter the risen Lord Jesus Christ, there is no excuse for not obeying His command to "go and tell." Choose to obey His command so that you can claim His promise and experience firsthand the impact of His presence and His power.

May

PRAYER

To My Children

The apostle Paul taught Timothy, his "beloved child," three things that we should be imparting to our children.

I recently have been thinking of the many things my parents taught me by their examples. And I wonder, What am I teaching my children by my example?

My parents taught me three things that I, in turn, want to teach my children. This Mother's Day, even though you may not have children of your own, ask God to whom you can impart these challenges. As far as we know, the apostle Paul didn't have children, but he referred to Timothy as his son (1 Corinthians 4:17). And Paul, by his example, taught Timothy the same three things my parents taught me.

Read 2 Timothy 1

DON'T BE AFRAID TO LIVE FOR JESUS

What phrase in 2 Timothy 1:7 implies Timothy was afraid? What reasons can you think of for his fear?

Give phrases from the following verses that imply fear: Numbers 13:31 – 14:23; 1 Samuel 17:20 – 24; John 12:42.

When have you been afraid for some of the same reasons? Do you think your children might also be afraid?

How does the psalmist comfort those who are afraid? See Psalm 27:1 – 3; 91:1 – 7; 118:6 – 7.

You are prayed for

How did Paul encourage Timothy in 2 Timothy 1:3? Give some ideas as to how Paul prayed for his fellow workers. See Ephesians 1:17 – 19; 3:16 – 19; Colossians 1:9 – 12.

When do you pray for your children? How do you pray? Write a prayer for each of them.

Have you ever told your children you are praying for them? If it's appropriate, this Mother's Day, give them the prayers you wrote for them.

According to Hebrews 7:22 – 25, who else is praying for your children? How? See John 17:20 – 26.

You are prepared

According to 2 Timothy 1:5 – 6, how was Timothy uniquely prepared to live for Christ?

Who have been your children's spiritual mentors?

What or who has God allowed into the life of your children that uniquely prepares them to live for Christ? Use Romans 8:28 to help pinpoint God's preparation and to encourage them.

You are empowered

According to Acts 1:8; Ephesians 3:20; and 2 Peter 1:3, what does God's power enable us to do?

Have your children had an experience of salvation through faith in Jesus Christ? If so, use the above verses to explain that God's power has been given — and that it simply needs to be acted upon.

Where was Timothy from, according to Acts 16:1? What example had Paul set for Timothy there that would lend credibility to Paul's words? See Acts 14:8 – 20.

How are you modeling your faith in Christ for your children?

Unashamed to share the gospel

What did Paul tell Timothy not to do in 2 Timothy 1:8?

What is the "testimony of our Lord" (KJV)? Give several fundamental elements from the following verses: Acts 3:12 – 21; 4:9 – 10; 1 Corinthians 15:3 – 8; Acts 1:9 – 11; Revelation 1:5 – 7.

When have you taught your children the basic tenets of the gospel?

When was the last time you shared the gospel with someone?

Unashamed to suffer for the gospel

Read Isaiah 64:6; Romans 3:23; John 14:6; Acts 4:12. Why do you think our Lord's testimony is offensive to our culture today?

If your children take a strong stand for our Lord's testimony, do you think they will increase in popularity? What does Paul say twice in 2 Timothy 1:8 – 12?

How can you encourage your children? See Joshua 1:9; Ephesians 6:10 – 18; Acts 4:20; Matthew 10:19 – 20; Jeremiah 1:7 – 9.

In spite of his suffering for the gospel, why did Paul say in 2 Timothy 1:12 that he was not ashamed to share it in the politically correct Roman Empire of his day?

How were Paul's words backed by the example of his life? See 2 Timothy 4:16 – 18; Acts 24:1 – 21; 25:23 – 26:29.

What are you teaching your children by your example?

DON'T BE APATHETIC TO LIVE FOR JESUS

Be committed to God's Word

How did Paul expound on the instructions he had given to Timothy earlier in his letter? See 2 Timothy 3:14 – 17.

When do you read your Bible? When have you instructed your children to read God's Word? What have you done to get your children started in a daily, systematic Bible study?

According to Psalm 119:9 – 11, 105, why is it important for your children to get into God's Word for themselves? Can you think of other reasons?

Be committed to God's work

How would you describe the work of Phygelus and Hermogenes in 2 Timothy 1:15? Give possible reasons for their actions.

How would you describe the work of Onesiphorus in 2 Timothy 1:16 – 18? How did it differ from that of Phygelus and Hermogenes?

How would you describe your work for Christ? Is it more similar to the work of Phygelus and Hermogenes or to Onesiphorus?

Have you ever walked away from God's work? If so, tell Him you're sorry and ask for another chance to serve. Compare Acts 15:36 – 38 with 2 Timothy 4:11.

How does 2 Timothy 4:7 – 8 describe the example Paul was setting for Timothy?

What can you do to teach your children to serve the Lord?

This Mother's Day, give your children the example of a parent who isn't afraid to live for Christ — be courageous! Give them the example of someone who is not ashamed of the gospel — be confident! And finally, give the example of someone who is not apathetic toward God's work or God's Word — be committed!

Every May many of us in the United States participate in the National Day of Prayer in which we are challenged to pray for our country. Regardless of where we live in the world, we all need to pray for our nation, and we are assured that God's blessing is conditioned on our prayers. But do you and I really know how and what to pray?

When I lack words in prayer or thoughts about how to pray, I turn to Scripture and use the words or patterns I find in the prayers of others. One prayer I have used in praying for my country is the one the prophet Daniel prayed long ago for his nation. Daniel was about ninety years old and still living in Babylonian captivity when he poured out his heart to God on behalf of his people.

Read Daniel 9:1 – 23

THE COMPULSION TO PRAY

Compelled by problems in the world

Based on the following verses, describe the Babylonians: Genesis 10:8 – 10; 11:1 – 9; 2 Kings 24:20 – 25:10.

Understanding that Daniel and his people were held in captivity in Babylon, describe some of the problems they faced.

What are some of the problems that your nation is facing today?

Why should problems compel us to pray? See Exodus 3:9 – 10; 2 Chronicles 7:13 – 14.

Compelled by promises in the Word

On what was Daniel's prayer based? How does this apply to your own prayer life? Are your prayers based on your wants — or on God's Word?

List the promises Daniel claimed from Jeremiah 25:12; 29:10 – 15.

What are some of the promises that you or I could claim for our own country? Consider 2 Chronicles 7:13 – 14. What other passages come to mind?

Read Deuteronomy 28. What are some of the promises, commands, and warnings to Israel that could also relate to your country?

What do you learn from Daniel's example as an old man in Daniel 9:1 – 3?

When do you pray for your country? How can you make this part of your regular prayer life?

THE COMMUNICATION IN PRAYER

Our concentration

Read Daniel 9:3. In order "to turn to the Lord," what do you think Daniel had to turn from? Relate this to Matthew 6:6; Luke 5:16; 6:12; 9:18.

In Matthew 6:16 – 18, what word did Jesus use that indicates fasting is not optional for you and me?

What do you learn from Elijah's example of prayer in 1 Kings 17:1; 18:42; James 5:16 – 18?

If fasting is going without something in order to make time to be alone with God in prayer, how does this help your concentration?

When do you fast? How can you make it a more consistent discipline in your life?

Our confidence

How does Hebrews 11:6 say we are to approach God?

What phrases from the following verses reveal Daniel's confidence in God's character? See Daniel 9:4, 7, 9, 15.

When you pray, do you expect God to hear and answer? On what basis?

What other prerequisite for confidence in prayer is mentioned in Hebrews 10:19 – 23?

Explain how you know you meet the New Testament prerequisite.

Our confession

What basic problem of his people did Daniel address in Daniel 9:5, 8 – 11? Give specific phrases.

How did this problem affect their relationship with God in Daniel 9:6 – 8?

How did this affect their national security? See Daniel 9:12 – 14.

How did this affect their relationship with other nations of the world? See Daniel 9:16.

Apply each of the above four answers to your own country.

Note the personal pronouns Daniel used in 9:4 – 16. Are they singular or plural?

How is this similar to Ezra's prayer for his people in Ezra 9:6 – 15?

From Ezra 9:5; 10:1 and Daniel 9:3, give the phrases that reveal the attitude of the one praying.

What does this teach you and me about how to pray for our people?

Our clarity

List the phrases that specify what Daniel is asking God to do in Daniel 9:16 – 19.

What fundamental reason does Daniel give God for answering his prayer in Daniel 9:19?

Write your specific requests for your country, based on Daniel's prayer.

THE CONFIRMATION OF PRAYER

How long did it take Daniel to receive confirmation that his prayer had been heard? See Daniel 9:20 – 21.

Do you think Daniel would have received insight into his people's national situation had he not prayed? See Daniel 9:20 – 22.

When was Daniel's prayer answered? See Daniel 9:23.

When did Daniel actually receive the answer to his specific requests? See Ezra 1:1 – 5.

Do you think Daniel's people would have been restored to God's place of blessing if Daniel had not prayed for them? See James 4:2; Jeremiah 10:21.

What conclusion can you draw from this Bible study about the importance of praying for your country?

Based on your prayers, how likely is it that God will bless your country?

Join with me in prayer: "Father, while we have been pointing our fingers at the sins of others, we feel the intense, fiery gaze of Your holiness directed at us — Your people. We choose now to humbly bow at the foot of the cross, to seek a fresh vision of who You are, and to pray. Our hearts are broken and contrite because of our own sin and that of our nation. As we specifically confess our sin, we ask that You hear our prayer, forgive our sin, and please, dear God ... bless our nation. In Jesus' name, Amen."

Do you have an unanswered prayer? Not just a small daily request, but a major heartbreaking, soul-wrenching, tear-soaking prayer that God has not answered? I do. And as I have wrestled with it, my thoughts at times have been in turmoil: Does God really love me? Has He heard me? Does He care? If He cares, is He unable to answer? Have I done something to displease Him? Why doesn't God answer my prayer? And I have been confronted with the temptation to blame God, to resent God, to turn away from God — to just stop praying because He doesn't seem to be answering anyway.[2]

As I have struggled with my "why?" I have sought answers in God's Word. With loving patience and gentle wisdom, He has led me to John 11 and the story of Martha's "unanswered prayer" in order to teach me to trust Him when I just don't understand.

---

2. This entry is based on *Why? Trusting God When You Don't Understand* by Anne Graham Lotz (Nashville: W, 2004). Used by permission.

UNANSWERED PRAYER DEVELOPS OUR FAITH

For this we need Jesus

From John 11:1 – 2, describe the family in Bethany and the crisis that arose.

In John 11:1 – 5, what attitude of Jesus toward this family is stated twice? Give the phrases.

Who or what is your "Lazarus"?

From John 11:3, put into your own words the implied "prayer" of Mary and Martha.

How did Jesus answer?

What did He do?

After bringing their request to Jesus, did the situation improve for Mary and Martha? What do you think of that?

How long has Jesus delayed after you have brought your request to Him?

Read John 11:14 – 15. What is astounding about Jesus' attitude toward Lazarus's death?

What insight does His attitude give us about our suffering?

From the following verses, what are some of His purposes for us in our suffering? See 1 Peter 1:6 – 7; 2 Corinthians 12:7 – 10; Hebrews 12:2; Revelation 1:9 – 13.

For this we have Jesus

According to John 11:17 – 20, what did Martha have in the midst of her suffering that the three Hebrew young men from Daniel 3:19 – 25 had in the midst of their trial?

Relate this to God's promise to us from Isaiah 43:1 – 4; Psalm 23:4 – 5.

How did Martha greet Jesus in John 11:21? Put it into your own words.

What have been some of your "if onlys"?

According to John 11:23, on what else could Martha base her faith in the midst of her suffering?

What promise has God given you in the midst of your suffering? Has your faith been based on "I hope so" or "He says so"?

In John 11:25 – 26, to what and to whom did Jesus direct Martha's attention?

Do you think Martha would have become this focused if she had not been desperate? How does this help answer why Jesus doesn't always give us what we want, when we want it?

The glory of His love

While similar, what is the difference between Martha's greeting of Jesus in John 11:21 – 22 and Mary's greeting in verse 32? Put it into your own words.

How did Jesus respond in John 11:33 – 35?

When have you invited Jesus to "come and see" your pain, your helplessness, your hopelessness, your despair?

Knowing He was going to raise Lazarus from the dead within moments, why do you think Jesus wept? See Isaiah 63:9; Hebrews 4:15; Psalm 56:8.

Why do you think we are told twice that Jesus was deeply moved? See John 11:33, 38.

Do you think Jesus saw a reflection of His own death and burial that would take place within the week? Relate this to Romans 5:8; Hebrews 12:2.

The glory of His lordship

What command did Jesus give Martha in John 11:39?

Why was obedience to this command unthinkable to Martha?

What stone is God commanding you to remove that is keeping your "Lazarus" buried? An unforgiving spirit? Anger? Pride? _____? Fill in the blank.

What was Martha's response to His command?

Did her resistance and argument speed or delay the deliverance of her loved one?

When Jesus seeks to do a miracle in the life of your loved one, what argument have you raised about His methods or His timing?

Could you be delaying a blessing because you are arguing?

What was Jesus' challenge to Martha in John 11:40? Put it into your own words. Relate this to James 2:26; John 5:8 – 9; 9:7; Mark 3:5.

If Martha truly believed, did she have any option but obedience? Why or why not?

What reason to obey did Jesus give Martha in John 11:40?

What reason do you need before you obey?

The glory of His life-giving power

Why did Jesus pray publicly before calling Lazarus forth from the tomb? See John 11:41 – 42.

When had that same voice been heard before? Compare John 1:1, 14 with Genesis 1:3; Luke 8:24 – 25, 49 – 55; Matthew 8:28 – 32.

What was the response to His voice in John 11:43 – 44?

Do you think His power has lessened or weakened over time? See Hebrews 13:6.

Read 2 Corinthians 12:7 – 10. What was the apostle Paul's "unanswered prayer"? How did it develop his faith and display God's glory?

Based on your brief study of John 11:1 – 44, write your own answer to "why?"

Remember … trust Him when you don't understand and nothing makes sense — after the cross come the resurrection and the glory and the crown. Keep your focus on the big picture and the ultimate goal: to live by faith in Jesus alone, that you and I might display His glory to an increasingly skeptical, cynical, hostile world!

Many people claim to speak for God. Do you know how to recognize which voice is authentic? Have you ever been confronted by someone who said something like "God told me to tell you ..."? Such statements often are followed by a "word of knowledge," such as, "If you only had more faith, you would be healed." Or, perhaps, "If you were living right, you would not have lost your job."

Someone, with compassion clothing the words, might even say, "God has told me that He doesn't mean for you to be unhappy. He would never want you to stay in this miserable marriage; He wants you to be happy." Or, "God has told me He wants you to be healthy (or wealthy or prosperous or problem-free)."

Such words spoken by sincere people within our circle of Christian friends can put us into a tailspin of emotional devastation and spiritual doubt. It is especially traumatic and confusing when those words are uttered by someone in a position of religious leadership.

How can you and I know which voice speaks the truth, which voice is authentic? Learning to recognize the voice of God is critical not only for our own peace of mind but also for developing a personal relationship with Him and for living a life pleasing to Him. Yet how can we be sure the voice we hear is His? Jesus answers that question using the illustration of the relationship between the shepherd and his sheep.

Read John 10:1 – 10

THE AUTHENTIC VOICE IS BIBLICAL

What does God say about the importance of determining which voice is authentic among the cacophony of voices clamoring for our attention? See Deuteronomy 18:18 – 20; Galatians 1:6 – 9.

What event in John 9 revealed that the religious leaders of Israel spoke with false voices as Jesus described?

In John 10:1 – 5, what are some of the criteria that Jesus gave for determining a false shepherd? A true shepherd? Give a practical application for each criterion.

THE AUTHENTIC VOICE IS PERSONAL

According to John 10:3 – 4, what is the basis of the relationship between the shepherd and his sheep?

In the parable Jesus gave, who is the shepherd? Who are the sheep? What is the shepherd's voice today? How do we, the sheep, hear His voice? Give an example of a time when you have heard the shepherd's voice.

According to John 10:5, why do the sheep run from the false shepherd? Give an example from your own life.

What is absolutely necessary if you and I are to discern between the voices of the true and the false shepherds?

How does the reaction of the religious leaders in John 10:6 reveal their identity as false shepherds?

THE AUTHENTIC VOICE IS POWERFUL

What is the Good Shepherd able to do that the false shepherd cannot? See John 10:7 – 10.

How does Jesus' claim disqualify the pluralism of our day? See John 10:7.

Give phrases from the following verses that confirm the uniqueness of Jesus' claim: John 1:1 – 3, 9, 14, 18; 3:2, 15 – 18; 14:6; Acts 4:12.

What practical steps will you take to make sure that the voice you are listening to is that of the Good Shepherd?

Ask God to give you more of His voice in your ear. Then listen … with your eyes on the pages of your Bible.

June

WISDOM

Eating Right to Stay Fit

I love junk food! Every year our family tries to go together to the North Carolina State Fair where we eat our way from one end to the other. Fried onions, hand-cut fried potato chips, fried pickles, fried Oreos, fried dough, fried Coke … I love anything fried! Except fried Snickers. Then there are candied apples, apple dumplings, cotton candy, roasted corn, hush puppies, apple cider, ham biscuits, funnel cakes, homemade ice cream, homemade milk shakes, homemade fudge … the list of culinary delights is endless! By the time I get home, I'm sick — very sick — and looking forward to next year's State Fair!

The orgy of junk food that is my once-a-year splurge at the State Fair would be extremely harmful if I made it a weekly or, even worse, a daily habit. Yet sometimes as Christians we all too often make a consistent diet of spiritual "junk food." We have made the main staples those things which have no real nutritional value — political agendas, social issues, human rights, books about God's Word, music videos, theological formulas for reaching the postmodernist, marketing strategies for the local church, along with a myriad of conferences, seminars, retreats, dramas, and "special events." None of these things are harmful in themselves, but when substituted for the nutrition of daily Bible reading and prayer, they make us spiritually "sick."

What does your spiritual "diet" consist of? Although you may be an active church member and a committed Christian, could it be that you are actually feasting on junk food while starving for the Bread of Life? It's time to start eating right!

Read John 6:30 – 40 and Exodus 16:1 – 21

According to John's gospel, Jesus had just fed more than 5,000 people with five loaves of bread and two fish. He now explains that the physical, material miracle has a personal, spiritual meaning.

THE LIVING BREAD — John 6.30 – 40

From John 6:30, what did the people ask Jesus for? Why did they ask Him for it?

What proof have you required from Jesus before you will fully commit yourself to Him?

The Bread is not earthly manna

On what Old Testament story did the Jews base their demand? See John 6:31.

When have you made a demand of God? What was it?

What do you think is the difference between making a demand and claiming a promise?

How do Christians today sometimes confuse their demands with God's promises?

In John 6:32 – 33, how did Jesus correct the people?

The Bread is a heavenly Man — Ex. 16:1 – 21

Describe the manna of Exodus 16:1 – 21 by answering the following questions; give verses for each of your answers.

    ✦ When was manna to be gathered?

    ✦ How often were God's children to gather it and how long could it be kept?

    ✦ Where did it come from?

    ✦ What difference did it make in the people's lives?

    ✦ What did a person have to do in order to benefit from it?

Who does the manna represent? See John 6:32 – 33.

Apply each aspect of your description of manna to Jesus Himself.

What earthly manna is substituted today for the heavenly Man?

THE LASTING BENEFITS

What do you think the people were really asking for in John 6:34?

How is the request of the people in John 6 similar to the request of the Samaritan woman in John 4:7 – 15?

Apply the request to things people ask Jesus for today.

Satisfaction

Define the "hunger" and "thirst" that Jesus speaks of in John 6:35. Compare Matthew 5:6.

How does He meet these needs in your life?

What does Philippians 4:13 say about this lasting benefit?

Acceptance

When have you experienced rejection? By whom?

How do Isaiah 53:1 – 6 and Hebrews 13:11 – 15 give you comfort and encouragement?

Describe the acceptance Jesus offers in John 6:37. Compare Matthew 27:44 with Luke 23:39 – 43; Ephesians 1:3 – 6; Revelation 22:4 – 5. What does this mean to you?

Security

Describe the security Jesus promises in John 6:38 – 39. See John 3:16; 10:27 – 30; Ephesians 1:13 – 14; Romans 8:31 – 39.

According to the above verses, what does your eternal security depend on?

Once you have placed your faith in Jesus Christ and been born again into the family of God, is there anything that can threaten or jeopardize your security? How does that make you feel?

Hope

What are some of the things people today are placing their hope in?

What are some popular opinions concerning what happens when a person dies?

Compare public opinion today with what Jesus said in John 6:40. What do the following verses have to say about that same hope? Compare Hebrews 9:27 with 1 Thessalonians 5:9 – 10; Job 19:26; John 11:25 – 26; 14:1 – 4; 1 Corinthians 15:12 – 22, 50 – 58; 1 Thessalonians 4:13 – 18; 1 Peter 1:3 – 5.

From John 6:47 – 51, what is one primary benefit of "eating right"? Explain in your own words what Jesus meant. See John 6:60 – 63.

What will you do today to improve your "diet"?

Filling your mind with wisdom that comes from studying the Scripture is better than enjoying the most festive food at any fair. So ... fill up on the Bread of Life and be sure to share your meal with others.

Loving Him . . .

We had just said good-bye to a radiant young bride-to-be. She had come to our house to tell my husband, my children, and me some of the exciting details of her upcoming wedding. Her eyes had been flashing, her smile sparkling, her dark glossy hair bouncing as her excitement spilled over her every word and gesture. As the door closed behind her, Rachel-Ruth, my youngest daughter, burst into tears and ran from the room! Morrow, my 10-year-old, was as astonished as I was. We bolted after Rachel-Ruth and found her sobbing in the living room. Her hands were frantically tearing at her long braids as though she would pull them from her little head and, between choking breaths, she said, "I hate my curly hair! I'm not pretty at all!" Morrow and I stared aghast at Rachel-Ruth. Then we burst into tears, threw our arms around her, and the three of us crumpled on the floor in a heap of despair! Over curly hair instead of straight hair! Over braided hair instead of bobbed hair! Over an 8-year-old body instead of a 21-year-old figure!

What ridiculous nonsense, you might say. But when you love someone with all your heart, that person's pain is yours. As her mother, I so empathize with Rachel-Ruth that her tears are mine.

Likewise, our heavenly Father so closely identifies with His children that our tears are His. And in response to such loyalty and love, I, in turn, desire to so closely identify with Him — with His grief, His joy, His love, His pain, His blessing, His honor — that His tears are on my face.

---

3. Portions of this Bible study were adapted from *My Heart's Cry* by Anne Graham Lotz (Nashville: W, 2002). Used by permission.

Read John 12:1 – 8

TEARS OF GRIEF

Read John 11:1 – 44 and explain why Mary wept in verse 33.

Jesus knew He would raise Lazarus from the dead. Given that, why do you think He wept? See John 11:35.

When was the last time you wept? Why were you weeping?

Give phrases from the following verses that show God cares about our pain: Isaiah 25:8; 40:1 – 2; 49:13; 53:4; Luke 4:18 – 21; 2 Corinthians 1:3 – 4.

TEARS OF JOY

Who were some of the guests at the dinner given in Jesus' honor, according to Matthew 26:6 – 8; John 12:2 – 4?

What was the reason for the dinner, according to John 12:1 – 2? Describe in your own words the emotions of Simon, Lazarus, Mary, and Martha.

When was the last time your gratitude for what God has done for you broke out into genuine celebration? Describe the contrast between the atmosphere in Simon's home and the turmoil brewing outside. See John 11:45 – 57; Mark14:10 – 11; John 12:9 – 11.

Relative to the way Jesus is acknowledged, talked about, and generally treated in today's society, how much of a contrast is there between what takes place in your home and what takes place outside its walls?

When was the last time you wept with joy over what God has done for you?

TEARS OF LOVE

From Luke 10:38 – 42 and John 11:28 – 32, describe Mary. How did she exemplify both faith and a failure to trust?

Describe the scene in John 12:1 – 3. Assuming Mary's jar of perfume was the equivalent to her life's savings and her dowry, what did it represent? What do you think motivated her to pour it all out on Jesus?

What is your most precious possession — your "alabaster jar"? Would you be willing to give it all to Jesus? If so, why?

From John 12:7, what did Jesus say was the underlying reason for Mary's sacrifice? Relate this to Philippians 3:10. Put into your own words what you think is meant by "the fellowship of sharing in His sufferings."

When have you shared Christ's cross?

How did others at the dinner party react to Mary's extravagant sacrifice? See John 12:4 – 5; Mark 14:4 – 5; Matthew 26:8 – 9. Put their reactions into your own words. How do you think they made Mary feel?

As you pour out the contents of your alabaster jar, has anyone ever made fun of your faith, criticized your commitment, faulted your service, or sneered at your love for Jesus, saying, in essence, "You're wasting your life, your time, your money" — on Him? How did it make you feel?

What was Jesus' response in Mark 14:6 – 9 to the harsh treatment of Mary? List at least four of His statements and put them into your own words.

How have you sensed God's pleasure in your sacrifice? What encouragement do you receive from the following verses: Psalm 51:16 – 17; Isaiah 57:15; Mark 10:29 – 30; Matthew 25:21; Hebrews 13:16?

Would you choose to love Jesus with His tears on your face? Reflect on His love for you.

In the early light of creation's dawn, the Father held His Alabaster Jar. It gleamed with the beauty of the Morning Star and was scented with the fragrance of the Rose of Sharon. It was His most precious possession. As His omniscient eyes looked down the years that stretched out before Him into generations and centuries and ages and millenniums, He knew . . .

The Father slipped into the darkness of the world He had made and loved. The hands that held the Jar — His Son — with such tender and eternal love relaxed and opened, as He placed the Jar ever so gently on the manger bed of hay. During the years that followed, the beauty and the glory of the Jar were shared and admired by those who had eyes to see.

And then the Father once again picked up His Alabaster Jar. And on a hill so far away from His celestial home — a hill that was cold, barren, and bleak, swarming with an angry mob that was unruly and obscene — the Father smashed His Alabaster Jar on a rugged wooden cross. As the contents of flesh and blood were all poured out and the fragrance of His love permeated human history forever, our tears were on His face.

The Risk of Faith

A cautious attitude in the spiritual realm can paralyze my faith or — at the least — cause me to procrastinate until obedience becomes a burden and walking by faith slows to a crawl. God has reminded me that He has not given me a "spirit of timidity, but a spirit of power."[4]

Living a life of faith requires taking risks, at least from our perspective, because we can't physically see what lies ahead, or hear what He's saying, or know what He's thinking, or feel what He's doing. We just have to trust Him moment by moment, day by day.

Read Exodus 1:1 – 2:10; Genesis 6:1 – 7; Daniel 3; and Matthew 14:22 – 33

GIVE UP OUR CHILDREN — Ex. 1:1 – 2:20

Describe the dangers that threatened the Levite woman's son when she placed him in the basket. See Exodus 2:1 – 3. How did God help her? See Exodus 2:5 – 9.

---

4. 2 Timothy 1:7.

If the Levite woman had not been willing to give up her son, what do you think would have happened to him? See Exodus 1:15 – 16, 22.

What dangers threatened Hannah's son when she left him at the temple? Compare 1 Samuel 1:24 – 28 with 2:12, 18, 22. How did God help Hannah? See 1 Samuel 2:21; 3:19 – 21.

What danger threatened Hagar's son in Genesis 21:12 – 16? How did God help Hagar? See Genesis 21:17 – 20.

What danger threatened Abraham's son in Genesis 22:1 – 2? How did God help Abraham? See Genesis 22:3 – 14.

What dangers threaten your child? What encouragement do you receive from the above examples?

What encouragement is there for parents in the following verses: Isaiah 40:11; 44:1 – 3; 54:13; Psalm 100:5?

GIVE UP OUR COMPLACENCY — Gen. 6:1 – 7

From Genesis 6:1 – 5, list as many characteristics as you can of the world in Noah's day, comparing each with our world today. See also Matthew 24:37 – 39.

Out of the entire world's population in Noah's day, how many people were right with God or even gave Him any serious thought? Give phrases from Genesis 6:1 – 9.

How could the world situation have caused Noah to be complacent?

Who do you know who has a wholehearted love for the Lord and their neighbor and who is following God in obedient discipleship? Who do you know who is not?

Describe our current culture. How has it affected your discipleship?

What do you think was the key to Noah's remaining faithful to God when everyone else was not? Give a phrase from Genesis 6:8 – 9.

What do you think the outcome would have been if Noah had been complacent?

Put the following commands into your own words, then apply each one to your own life: 1 John 1:5 – 7; 2:6, 15 – 17; 2 Corinthians 5:16 – 18.

How does obedience to these commands help you to avoid complacency?

GIVE UP OUR COMPROMISE — Dan. 3:1 – 30

Who was invited to the dedication of the king's image in Daniel 3:1 – 3?

What was the "safe" thing to do, according to Daniel 3:4 – 16?

Describe the choice of the three Hebrew men. How hard must it have been for them to make that choice, in light of the choices their peers were making?

What were the immediate consequences of their choice in Daniel 3:8 – 13?

How was the pressure to compromise increased in Daniel 3:14 – 15? How did the Hebrews respond? Write in your own words the king's challenge in verse 15 and the Hebrews' response in verses 16 – 18.

Who is pressuring you to compromise? How have they increased the pressure? What has been your response?

Did God save the three Hebrews from being thrown into the fire? Describe how they must have felt in Daniel 3:19 – 24.

What does God promise when you go through disaster, disease, disappointment, and difficulty? Give phrases from the following verses: Psalm 23:4; Isaiah 43:1 – 2; Deuteronomy 31:6, 8; Joshua 1:9; Jeremiah 1:8; Psalm 139:7 – 12, 17 – 18; Zephaniah 3:17.

If the three Hebrews had compromised, what would they have gained? What would they have lost? See Daniel 3:25 – 30.

How does Matthew 16:24 – 26 address this?

GIVE UP OUR COMFORT — Matt. 14:22 – 33

Why were the disciples in the boat on the lake during a storm? See Matthew 14:22.

From the following verses, show how it's possible to be in a "storm" while at the same time in God's will: 2 Corinthians 11:23 – 27; 2 Timothy 3:10 – 12; 1 Peter 4:16, 19; Revelation 1:9.

What storm are you in? Do you think it is evidence that you are not in God's will? Or that He is not pleased with you? Or that He doesn't care about you?

Describe Peter's probable comfort level in a boat — storm or not. See Luke 5:1 – 3; Matthew 4:18; John 21:1 – 3.

What opportunity did Peter have in the storm that he wouldn't have had any other way? See Matthew 14:28 – 29. Relate this to 1 Peter 1:6 – 9.

Tell at least two things Peter had to do in order to take the opportunity.

Using your imagination, describe how Peter might have felt and what he might have seen initially as he stepped out of the boat.

Do you think taking this opportunity was easy for Peter?

What did Peter risk by stepping out of the boat?

Why do you think the other disciples did not take the same opportunity? What did they miss that Peter obviously received?

What is your "boat" or your comfort zone?

Apply John 10:2 – 4, 11 to your own life.

If you play it safe, make a list of the things you will gain and the things you will lose.

How do you think each of the characters in our study would reply if you could ask them, "Was taking the risk of faith worth it in the long run?" I believe they would all answer, "Yes! Yes! Yes!"

Take the risk of faith so that at the end of your life you can also say, "I received a hundredfold return on anything I ever gave up. Taking the risk was more than worth it! Because He is worth it!"

Check Your Foundation

Several years ago my husband and I asked a contractor to examine the foundation of our house to determine if it was strong enough to withstand new construction. He reported that the pilings had so weakened that anyone who walked across the floor above them would fall through. Without hesitation, we decided to rebuild the old pilings and thus strengthen the foundation of our home.

The foundation of our society at large, and of our lives, in particular, needs to be reexamined too. Is it strong enough for the new construction — the advances in science, technology, and medicine that are opening before us in the twenty-first century?

We hear a lot about the "pilings" which we sometimes call "values": family values, ethical values, moral values, medical values, individual values, religious values. But when was the last time you examined them as they undergird the foundation of your own life and family and business? Observing our culture, "Whatever makes you happy or works for you or feels good" seems to be a generally accepted value. But is that what the Bible teaches?

It's time to check your foundation. Which pilings are weak?

According to Exodus 20:1, where do the values in this chapter come from?

Give a phrase from each of the following verses that underscores the source of our values: Deuteronomy 5:12, 15, 16, 22, 32 – 33.

What gives God the right to establish our values? See Genesis 1:1.

THE FOUNDATION OF SPIRITUAL VALUES

God should be preeminent — Ex. 20:3

As you consider Exodus 20:3, what are some other gods that are commonly placed first in our lives? See 1 Timothy 6:10; Luke 21:34; 1 Peter 4:3; Jeremiah 45:5.

In Matthew 22:37 – 38, how does Jesus confirm and restate the value of putting God first?

What action will you take to strengthen this foundational "piling" of giving God preeminence in your life?

God should be worshiped — Ex. 20:4

As you consider Exodus 20:4, how can you improve the clarity of your focus on God? See Job 33:26; Psalm 14:2; 119:11; John 1:18; 2 Timothy 2:19.

Explain what Jesus meant in John 4:24.

Are you the kind of worshiper that God seeks? See John 4:22 – 23.

God should be honored — Ex. 20:7

How do Leviticus 19:12 and 22:32 reaffirm this value presented in Exodus 20:7?

What do you think it means to profane God's name?

When you call yourself a Christian but don't act like one, what happens to God's good name?

God should be followed — Ex. 20:8

As you consider God's command in Exodus 20:8, how did He set the example for us in Genesis 2:2 – 3?

Give phrases from Exodus 20:9 – 11 that refer to the basis for this value.

In your own words, what does Isaiah 58:13 – 14 say about how to apply this value to our daily life and about the blessings of following God's example in our weekly schedule?

What will you do to set apart one day a week to follow God more closely?

THE FOUNDATION OF SOCIAL VALUES

Family relationships are important — Ex. 20:12

According to Ephesians 6:1 and 1 Timothy 5:4, what is one way to obey God's command in Exodus 20:12 to honor our parents?

How are we to guard and interact with family members, according to Luke 17:3; Romans 14:10, 13; 1 Corinthians 8:13; 1 Thessalonians 4:6; James 4:11; 1 John 4:21; 5:16; Mark 3:35?

What will you do to improve your family relationships?

Human life is sacred — Ex. 20:13

What is the basis for the sacredness of human life? See Genesis 1:27; Exodus 20:13.

Recognizing that all human life is sacred, how are we to treat others? See Acts 10:34; Ephesians 4:2, 32; Luke 6:31; Romans 12:10; 13:8; Galatians 5:13; 1 Peter 3:8.

If you have not treated others as you should, what hope is there for you, according to 1 Corinthians 6:9 – 11?

What difference would it make in the way you treat others if you viewed each person as one of inestimable eternal worth — someone God created, loved, and died for?

Sex has limits — Ex. 20:14

Read Genesis 2:20 – 25; Exodus 20:14. How does knowing that God thought of sex in the first place affect your view of sex?

How does Jesus affirm God's idea in Matthew 19:4 – 6?

What limits has God placed on sex? See Leviticus 18:5 – 30; 1 Corinthians 6:9, 18; 7:2; Jude 7.

What are some practical things you can do to not only maintain your sexual purity but to help your children maintain theirs?

Honesty is the best policy — Ex. 20:15

God condemns stealing (dishonest behavior in all its forms) in Exodus 20:15. Where does Jesus say that such behavior originates? See John 8:44.

Where does such behavior lead? See Revelation 21:8.

What are some of the benefits of being honest, according to Psalm 25:21; Proverbs 11:3; 13:6?

How is Jesus' example in Matthew 22:16 to be reflected in your own life, according to Titus 2:7 – 8?

Say what you mean, and mean what you say — Ex. 20:16

God condemns false witness or testimony in Exodus 20:16. How does this "piling" reach all the way to heaven? See Isaiah 45:23; John 1:1, 14; 14:6.

How are your words to reflect His? See Matthew 5:37; James 5:12; 1 Peter 4:11.

What do you think are the "empty words" of Ephesians 5:6 and 1 Thessalonians 2:5? The controversial words in 1 Timothy 6:4 and 2 Timothy 2:14? The powerless words in Colossians 2:4?

Take a moment now and pray Psalm 19:14 for yourself.

Be content with what you have — Ex. 20:17

God condemns covetousness in Exodus 20:17. What is the source of your contentment, according to Proverbs 19:23?

How does your relationship with God directly affect your peace of mind? See Hebrews 13:5; Philippians 4:11 – 12; 1 Timothy 6:6.

While I am distressed that our society is offended by the public posting of the Ten Commandments — our "foundational pilings" — I believe God is more concerned that you and I read them, study them, apply them, and live by them. Today, begin writing them on the tablet of your heart.

How to Seek God's Guidance

Often I am asked, "Anne, I have a major decision to make. How can I know if it is in God's will?" In response, I usually begin by explaining that when an airplane comes in to land during the night, the controller tells the pilot to line up the runway lights. When the lights are kept in a straight line, the pilot can be assured of landing in the center of the runway.

When you and I are making a decision "in the dark," we also can line up the "runway lights" that assure us our decision is in the center of God's will. The four runway lights that I use to determine God's will in making a decision are:

1. The confirmation of God's Word.
2. My inner conviction.
3. Practical circumstances.
4. The counsel of godly, mature Christian friends.

In Acts 10, Peter made a major decision that has affected the church to this day. In Acts 11, Peter explained his decision to the church leaders in Jerusalem. See if you can line up his "runway lights."

Read Acts 10:1 – 11:18

Describe in your own words the decision that Peter made in Acts 10 that then had to be explained to the Jerusalem church leaders in Acts 11.

THE CONFIRMATION OF GOD'S WORD — Acts 11:4 – 10

What did God say to Peter that related to his decision? See Acts 11:4 – 10.

What Bible verses or passages have come to you — during your daily devotions, Bible study, or through a sermon — that relate to your decision? Make a list with references and content.

As you read the Scripture that you have written out, does it seem to indicate one course of action over another?

THE CONVICTION OF YOUR SPIRIT — Acts 11:12

What phrase in Acts 11:12 indicates that Peter felt deep within himself he was to make this decision?

What do you believe in your heart is God's will for your situation?

What practical circumstances seemed to fall into place for Peter? See Acts 11:11, 13–17.

What doors of opportunity opened immediately for him?

How did subsequent events confirm the decision he made?

Make a list of the practical circumstances surrounding your call. What doors of opportunity seem to be opening?

What counsel is implied in Acts 10:23 and in Acts 11:12?

How did the initial reaction of the church leaders seem to contradict the earlier counsel and Peter's decision? See Acts 11:1–3, 18.

After hearing Peter relate the details of his decision, what was the leaders' final response?

List the names of two or three mature Christians who know you. Go over your answers to the above questions with them. Ask them to prayerfully give you wise counsel concerning your decision.

PUTTING IT TOGETHER

In order to step out in faith, confident that your decision is in God's will, you should have at least three of the four runway lights in place.

Sometimes, practical circumstances don't seem to line up. God may be testing you, requiring you to take a step of faith before things work out. When the children of Israel crossed the Jordan River, they had to get their feet wet before the waters rolled back.[5] But if God closes the door, you cannot force it open,[6] so don't try to manipulate circumstances to make your decision work.

At other times, you may be unable to discern your inner conviction, or you may not feel strongly one way or another about a specific direction. But as you begin to walk by faith, increasingly you should have a deep inner confidence that your decision is of God.

It may be that your Christian friends disagree with your decision. Or you may not know several godly people to whom you can go for wise counsel. As a result, this runway light will not line up. However, as you begin to follow through on your decision, mature Christians should confirm it.

When one of the above runway lights is missing, it is still possible to step out in faith. But the one runway light that is indispensable is the confirmation of God's Word. You must have it — no exceptions. God's Word can come to you in various ways: through your daily devotions or Bible study, through a sermon, through a verse that comes to mind while praying, or through searching the Scriptures specifically for it. But in order to be assured that your decision is in God's will, you must have His Word to confirm it.

I am cautious of formulas, but I can testify from years of experience that these runway lights work. So ... line yours up! Step out in faith! Ask and trust God to shut the door if for some reason you have misread His direction. He has promised to guide the meek — those who have no agendas of their own but simply desire to walk in the center of His will.[7] Get going! Land the "plane" of your life safely.

---

5. See Joshua 3:15 – 16.
6. See Revelation 3:7.
7. See Psalm 25:9.

July

REVIVAL

The River of Life

Our state recently endured a severe drought. Our shrubbery dropped their leaves and died, our green grass turned brown and crispy, and we operated under city-issued water restrictions. The water reservoir that serves our county dried to nothing more than a mudflat. The dusty, polluted air was of such poor quality that warnings to remain indoors were issued day after day. We desperately needed rain, and lots of it.

The shortage of water gave me a glimpse of what many people around the world endure on a daily basis. We all have seen pictures of emaciated people standing in line under a blistering sun, dust swirling around them, as they patiently wait with a bucket for a few cups of rationed water. Water is essential to life. It's that simple.

It's no wonder, therefore, that throughout the Bible, water symbolizes that which is essential to spiritual life and health. In the very last chapter of the Bible, an angel directs the attention of the apostle John to a river that runs through the center of our heavenly home ... a river that symbolizes the fact that our Father's house is saturated in "water."

THE SIGNIFICANCE OF THE RIVER

What was the significance of a river in Genesis 2:10?

Describe the characteristics of the river from Isaiah 55:1 – 2; Ezekiel 47:1 – 9; John 4:13 – 14; 7:37 – 38.

What are the similarities between the river in Revelation 22 and the river in Ezekiel 47? Are there any differences?

What do you think the river symbolizes? Base your answer on Scripture.

THE SOURCE OF THE RIVER — Rev. 22:1

Where does the river originate? See Ezekiel 47:1 – 2; Revelation 22:1.

What does the altar represent? See Exodus 30:20; Deuteronomy 27:6; Isaiah 56:7; Genesis 22:1 – 2, 9 – 18 with John 19:17 – 18; Romans 12:1 – 2.

What does the throne represent? See 1 Kings 22:19; Psalm 9:7; 11:4; Isaiah 6:1; Ephesians 1:20 – 22; Revelation 4:1 – 2.

Is there a single source for this river or are there several sources? Base your answer on Scripture.

As you combine what you understand about the significance and the source of the river, how does this apply to your life today?

The depths of saturation

From Ezekiel 47:3 – 5, to what four depths did the man go into the river?

How would you apply each depth to your own experiences? When have you been up to your ankles, knees, waist, and when have you been in over your head?

When you are swimming in the river, what part of your body can be seen by others? With this in mind, why do you think it's important to make Christ the head of your life? See Ephesians 1:22 – 23. Relate this to Ezekiel 47:5; John 7:37 – 39; Ephesians 5:18.

At what depth in the river are you today? At what depth do you want to be?

The delights of saturation

From Revelation 22:2, what is the first blessing the river produces? Relate this to Genesis 2:9; 3:24; John 3:16.

What is the second blessing the river produces? Relate this to Galatians 5:22 – 23; Colossians 3:12 – 17.

What is the third blessing the river produces? Relate this to Isaiah 53:4 – 5; Revelation 21:4.

What does the "curse" represent in Revelation 22:3? See Genesis 3:14 – 19; Romans 3:23; 6:23; 1 Corinthians 15:54 – 57.

What four things are a direct result of the "curse" being removed? See Revelation 22:3 – 5.

Is there any possibility that the river does not exist? Or that saturation in the river does not produce blessing? See Revelation 22:6.

Do you think the delights of saturation are directly related to the depths you are saturated? Base your answer on Scripture.

Where are you in relation to the river? Are you still on the riverbank, complaining that you are spiritually "dry"? Have you gingerly tested the "waters" without making the commitment to step into the river? Would you plunge in without reservations, asking God to give you all He has for you? Then invite someone else to go "swimming" with you.

The Cross

Every year on July 4 the United States celebrates our nation's birthday — our national day of independence. As terrorists seem to grow more bold and blatant, as wars seem to rumble and reproduce, as desert dictators spread long and tenacious tentacles, I praise God for the blessing of living in a free, democratic society! Whenever I fly around New York City, so aware of the vacancy in the skyline where the World Trade Center towers once stood, I strain to catch a glimpse of the Statue of Liberty in the harbor, lifting her torch as a beacon of freedom to the world. The sight never ceases to move me to thank God and ask Him to continue to bless this nation.

There is another "Statue of Liberty" for which I thank God. Although I have never seen it with my physical eyes, it has affected my life much more than the "lady" in New York Harbor. It is the cross. And the vision of it never ceases to move me to thank God afresh for setting me free from self, sin, and the power of Satan.

FREEDOM FROM SELF

"Self" is our old nature — emotions, will, and intellect — that is outside of Christ. What other terms are used to describe this nature in Romans 7:18; Ephesians 4:22; Colossians 3:5?

In Romans 8:1, what does the "therefore" refer to? See Romans 7:21 – 25. Relate this to Galatians 5:1.

In what way have you either failed or been frustrated in your effort to live a life pleasing to God? Describe your experience.

Understanding that the "law of sin and death" in Romans 8:2 is the cycle of failure and frustration that often besets us, what three actions must we take to experience freedom from it? See Acts 2:38 with Romans 8:11; 8:4.

What does it mean to "not live according to the sinful nature" in Romans 8:4? See Romans 8:7.

What does it mean to "live according to the Spirit"? See Romans 8:5; Galatians 5:16 – 18; Colossians 3:2; Philippians 2:1 – 11; 4:8. Is this optional for the Christian's life? See Romans 8:8.

FREEDOM FROM SIN

According to 1 Peter 4:2, what is the focus of our "self"? What does it produce, according to 1 Peter 4:3? Galatians 5:19 – 21? Colossians 3:5 – 9?

How does Romans 6:12, 16, 20 – 21 describe a life lived according to our "self," or old nature? How dangerous is this deliberately sinful lifestyle, according to Galatians 5:21? Hebrews 10:26 – 31? Revelation 21:8; 21:27?

Give phrases from the following verses that describe the defensive action we need to take in order to experience freedom from sin: 1 John 1:8 – 9; 2:1; Romans 8:13; Colossians 3:5, 7; Galatians 5:24; Ephesians 4:22 – 23. Describe the offensive action: Galatians 5:1, 13, 16; Ephesians 4:24; Romans 6:11 – 13.

For what are we encouraged to give thanks, according to Romans 6:17 – 18?

From the following verses, make a list of other things to be thankful for regarding freedom from the power of sin: 1 John 1:7, 9; Galatians 2:20; Romans 6:22 – 23; Romans 8:1 – 3; 1 Corinthians 6:11; Ephesians 1:7; 2:13; Revelation 1:5.

FREEDOM FROM SATAN

Who is Satan? Compare Luke 10:18 with Isaiah 14:12 – 15.

Is Satan a created being? See Colossians 1:15 – 16.

Under whose authority does he operate? See Luke 4:33 – 36; Ephesians 1:19 – 22.

Who is Satan in regard to the believer, according to Ephesians 6:11 – 12; 1 Peter 5:8?

Do you think he has the advantage if you refuse to acknowledge that he exists? Did Jesus believe Satan exists? See Luke 4:1 – 13.

From the following verses, how do we experience freedom from Satan? See 1 Peter 5:9; Ephesians 4:27; 6:10 – 18; James 4:7; Revelation 12:11.

What has been made possible for us, now that Satan's power has been broken by the cross, according to 1 John 3:7 – 8; Hebrews 2:14 – 15; 1 Corinthians 15:54 – 57?

What is Satan's ultimate fate, according to Revelation 20:10?

Until the day Satan is destroyed, how do the following verses encourage you? See 2 Kings 6:8 – 23; 1 John 4:4.

What can you do now to experience freedom from Satan, according to James 4:7; 1 Peter 5:8 – 9; Ephesians 6:11 – 18?

What will you do to set your mind on the things of the Spirit?

What sin will you put off so that you can put on the counterpart that is a characteristic of Christ?

How will you maintain your weapons of daily prayer and Bible reading, as well as your armor, so that you can live in the "freedom for which Christ has set us free"?

Celebrate liberty! Praise God for setting you free through the work of Jesus Christ on the cross! You are truly free at last!

Why Did Jesus Die?

Have you ever heard someone say that there are other ways to God besides Jesus? That all religions are equal? That as long as we are sincere in what we believe, a loving God will accept us? That the cross was not necessary? That if our good works outweigh our bad works, we can hope to go to heaven?

At a World Economic Forum in Davos, Switzerland, I heard a Muslim imam say that he did not believe in vicarious atonement for sin. In other words, he did not believe the death of Jesus was necessary or that the cross was necessary.

If he's right and there are other ways to God besides Jesus — if all religions are equal, if God accepts all those who are sincere in their beliefs, if our good works earn us a ticket to heaven — then why did Jesus have to die?

If there had been any other way to offer us forgiveness of sin, to reconcile us to God, to give us eternal life, and to open heaven for us when we die, God would have found it. But there is no other way.

Read John 18 and 19

JESUS DIED TO FORGIVE ANYONE

Even those who doubt Him

What did Annas, the former high priest, question Jesus about? See John 18:19.

Apply Annas's questions to doubts people have today.

What did Caiaphas question? See Matthew 26:63.

Apply Caiaphas's question and dramatic denial of Jesus' answer (and the response from Caiaphas) in Matthew 26:64 – 66 to people's doubts today.

What doubts do you have about God's Word or about who Jesus is?

Read Matthew 14:31; 21:21; Mark 11:23; James 1:6. Why is it important to resolve your doubts?

Would you confess your doubts to Jesus, ask His forgiveness, and then place your faith in Him and in His Word?

Even those who deny Him

Describe Peter's confidence in Matthew 26:31 – 35.

Describe his denial of Jesus in Matthew 26:69 – 75.

Use the following verses to describe why you think Peter repeatedly denied Jesus when he had been clearly warned and had sworn that he would not: Proverbs 11:2; 16:18. Compare Mark 14:32 – 38 with Proverbs 6:9 – 11.

What are some things that you and I can do to guard against this sin? See Psalm 56:3 – 4; 1 Peter 4:7; 1 Corinthians 16:13.

What wisdom does Peter share from his own experience in 1 Peter 5:8 – 9?

How do we deny Jesus today?

Describe a time when you have denied Christ. Would you confess it to Him now and ask for His forgiveness?

Even those who reject Him

Relate John 1:11 to Matthew 26:57 – 67.

Relate John 1:10 to John 19:1 – 16.

Who do you know who has rejected Jesus?

What encouragement do you find in the following Scripture passages: Acts 2:22 – 24, 36 – 41; 3:13 – 15; 4:4?

If you have rejected Jesus, what do you need to do? See Acts 3:19 – 20; John 1:12. What is keeping you from doing it now?

Consider 1 John 1:8 – 10. What is your sin? Would you confess it, using the same name for it that God does, and ask Him to cleanse you with the blood of Jesus?

His death is our sacrifice

From the following verses, describe what God's law required in order for a sinner to obtain forgiveness: Leviticus 5:5 – 6, 17 – 19; 17:11.

Read Hebrews 10:1 – 4. Did the sacrifices under the old covenant really take away sin? If not, why were they required?

How was the sacrificial law an audiovisual aid of who Jesus is and what He would do? Give phrases from Isaiah 53:4 – 12; John 1:29; Romans 3:22 – 25; Hebrews 13:11 – 12; 1 John 4:10.

Is there any other sacrifice for sin we can offer that God will accept?

When have you claimed Jesus as God's sacrifice for your sin?

His death is our substitute

Describe God's instructions to Moses in Exodus 12:1 – 7, 12 – 13, noting key phrases. What two things were necessary to secure salvation from God's judgment?

As though speaking to someone outside the church, or to a child, explain how the Passover is a picture of Jesus. Use these passages to help you: Matthew 26:2; 1 Corinthians 5:7; 1 Peter 1:18 – 19.

Read Revelation 5:1 – 13; 7:9 – 17; 12:10 – 11; 21:1 – 2, 22 – 23; 22:3. How relevant to your future is the word picture in these passages? Explain.

When judgment comes, either at your death or when Jesus returns, will it pass over you? Why?

His death is sufficient

Read Hebrews 10:5 – 14, 17 – 18. What further sacrifice does God require for our sin?

How is this confirmed by Jesus' own words spoken from the cross in John 19:30?

When you claim the sacrifice of Jesus Christ, what sin is forgiven? Give phrases from the following: 1 John 1:7, 9; 2:2, 12; Ephesians 1:7; Colossians 2:13 – 15. Apply each phrase to your own life.

Besides obtaining God's forgiveness, what other blessings does the blood of Jesus secure for the believer? See Revelation 1:5 – 6; Hebrews 10:19 – 22; Romans 5:9; Colossians 1:19 – 20.

Right now thank God for sending His only beloved Son to die on the cross as His sacrifice for your sin. Thank Him by confessing your sin and living humbly in His forgiveness. Then go and tell someone else why Jesus died.

The Good News of the Gospel

One day I received a call inviting me to be the keynote speaker at the leadership convention of a large national Christian organization. When I asked why I was being invited to do this, the man on the other end of the telephone line said, "Because we know you have a heart for the gospel."

As I hung up the phone, I wondered how the man could have known that about me. I concluded, of course, that the assumption was made because I was Billy Graham's daughter. But I began soul-searching for a few days, asking God not only to enlarge my heart for the gospel but also to help me understand more clearly just what the gospel is.

How would you answer if someone asked you, "What is the gospel?" The following verses helped me to define it more clearly, to declare it more boldly, and to defend it more firmly. I pray that they will help you in the same way.

Read Romans 1:16 – 18

DEFINING THE GOSPEL

Use one or more phrases from each of the following verses to define the gospel: Romans 3:23; 3:10; 1:18; 6:23; John 3:16; 1 John 1:9; Revelation 3:20; John 1:12; Ephesians 1:13; 2:8 – 9; 2 Corinthians 5:17.

Read Peter's sermon at Pentecost in Acts 2:14 – 36, at the temple in Acts 3:12 – 26, and to the religious leaders in Acts 4:8 – 12. Give the main points, with verses, that are the same in each sermon. How do these main points define the gospel?

List the phrases from Luke 24:1 – 7 that contain these same points.

Write in your own words a definition of the gospel for someone who has never heard it.

DECLARING THE GOSPEL

Why was Paul obligated to declare the gospel? Compare Romans 1:14 to 1 Timothy 1:12 – 16. To whom did he declare the gospel in Romans 1:16? Is anyone excluded from it? Support your answer with phrases from John 3:16 and Acts 4:12.

Judging from Romans 1:15 – 16 and 2 Timothy 1:8 – 12, what was Paul's attitude about declaring the gospel?

What was Peter's attitude about declaring the gospel in Acts 4:20?

What was the attitude of the early Christians toward declaring the gospel? See Acts 4:18 – 31; 5:40 – 42.

How does Paul describe you and me in 2 Corinthians 5:20?

What is your attitude toward declaring the gospel?

Pinpoint the time, the place, and the person with whom you last shared the gospel. Pray now and ask God to give you the opportunity this week to define and to declare the gospel to someone who doesn't know it.

As you pray and then look for opportunities to share the gospel, what encouragement do you receive from the promises in Luke 21:15 and 2 Thessalonians 2:16 – 17?

DEFENDING THE GOSPEL

How does Jude 3 challenge us to defend the gospel?

Why is this defense necessary, according to Jude 4 and 18?

How does Paul challenge us in 2 Timothy 1:13 – 14 to defend the gospel?

What warning do we need to heed in Galatians 1:3 – 9?

What are some "other gospels" being preached today?

How do we defend the gospel, according to Ephesians 6:10 – 18?

Why is sharing the gospel so difficult? See 1 Corinthians 1:23; 2 Timothy 4:3 – 5; Ephesians 6:12; 1 Peter 5:8.

What is our Lord's command in Mark 16:15? Is obedience optional?

Read 1 John 4:4 – 6; 5:3 – 5. What promises does God give to those who are obedient? What insights? What encouragement?

In a politically correct, inclusive, tolerant culture that says there are many gods and that all religions are equal, it's time for you and me to define, declare, and defend the gospel of Jesus Christ. Just do it!

Come to Jesus

Ever since I was a young girl, I have yearned to feel God's hand on my life, to make an eternal difference in the lives of others, to be used for His glory. I have wanted my life to have eternal significance. God has given me the desire of my heart by opening doors of opportunity for me to serve Him inside and outside of my home.

As I reflect back over the years, His call stands out in sharper focus. And it's not as complicated as I've tried to make it at times — because He has called me, very simply, to just come to Jesus.

Read 1 Corinthians 1:8 – 9

COME . . . TO SEE THE FACE OF GOD

Rewrite the verses in 1 Corinthians 1:8 – 9 and insert your name where appropriate.

Read John 14:8 – 11. What did Philip ask Jesus? What was Jesus' answer?

How did the apostle John affirm this amazing truth in John 1:18?

Read Exodus 3:1 – 6, 13 – 14. How did God identify Himself to Moses? How did Jesus identify Himself in the same way in John 8:53 – 58?

What is the thrilling promise given to every believer in Revelation 22:4?

COME . . . TO SEE THE GLORY OF GOD

What was Moses' request in Exodus 33:18? How did God answer his request in Exodus 33:19 – 34:8?

Consider Exodus 33. How would you define God's glory? How is this same definition also implied in John 1:14?

Read Isaiah 6:1 – 4. Whom did Isaiah say he saw? Give a phrase-by-phrase description.

In John 12:41, who did John say Isaiah saw?

What is another aspect of God's glory, according to Mark 9:2 – 3?

How is this aspect described in Hebrews 1:1 – 3?

COME . . . TO EXPERIENCE THE POWER OF GOD

Describe the circumstances in Matthew 14:22 – 24. How did the circumstances get worse in verses 25 – 26?

What storm is buffeting your life? How has it been worsened by your own worry and fear?

According to Matthew 14:27, what did Jesus give to His disciples in the midst of the storm?

In the very next verse, how did Peter use this situation to experience the power of God in his life?

What did Jesus say to Peter in Matthew 14:29?

How can you use your stormy circumstances to step out in faith and experience the power of God?

COME . . . TO FIND THE PURPOSE OF GOD

What were Peter and Andrew doing when Jesus called them and revealed His purpose for their lives in Matthew 4:18 – 20?

What did they have to do before they could live out God's purpose for their lives?

Do you think you have to be in a church or in a Bible study — or even in prayer — in order to discover God's purpose for your life?

What are you doing today? Could God be calling you today — now — to just come and follow Jesus?

What did Jesus say when Peter compared his call to John's in John 21:18 – 22?

In what ways are you dissatisfied with God's call on your life because you are comparing it to someone else's? What do you need to do?

COME . . . TO ENJOY THE PEACE OF GOD

What are your burdens? What is making your spirit tired?

According to Matthew 11:28 – 30, what is the antidote for this kind of weariness?
Write the personal encouragement you receive from Matthew 11:28 – 30; Mark 6:30 – 32; Philippians 4:6 – 7; 1 Peter 5:7.

What can you do today and how can you rearrange your schedule for tomorrow in order to get alone with Jesus?

What did Jesus promise the Samaritan woman in John 4:4 – 14?

Read John 7:37 – 39. What do you think Jesus meant by "living water," and what must you do to receive it?

How is this similar to the "bread of life" in John 6:35, 50 – 51, 57 – 63?

Who is the Spirit referred to in these passages, according to John 14:16 – 17, 25 – 26; 16:7 – 15?

When do you drink of the "living water"? When do you eat of the "bread of life"?

See Revelation 22:17. What thrilling invitation is the climaxing crescendo of the entire Bible?

COME . . . JUST AS YOU ARE

Describe the condition of each of the following people who came to Jesus: Mark 1:40 – 42; 2:3 – 12; 5:1 – 20, 25 – 29; 7:31 – 35; 8:22 – 25; 10:13 – 16. Apply each physical condition to a spiritual condition today.

What did each of these people have to do before they came to Jesus?

What do you have to do in order to come to Jesus?

Would you accept God's invitation? Would you answer God's call?

As the world unravels and our culture collapses, would you come to Jesus?

As blasphemous bestselling books are made into blasphemous box-office hits, would you come to Jesus?

As disease strikes your body and death claims your loved one and divorce divides your family and depression knocks on the door of your mind, would you come to Jesus?

Come to Jesus ... come to Jesus *now* ... and bring someone else with you.

August

REST

A Lasting Vacation

Each summer I find myself looking forward to spending one week at the beach with my family. I take long walks at sunrise, have my quiet times on the porch with a bottomless cup of coffee, relax in the sun while watching everyone else play and bodysurf the waves, serve hot suppers topped off with homemade ice cream and pound cake, then return home rested, refocused and restored — for about a week. While the memories last a lifetime, the "vacation" lasts only a few days.

It's obvious I need something more than just a one-week break from day-to-day pressures. I need a vacation that lasts — a vacation that is built into the framework of my life and permeates everything else. I need a vacation that gives me personal satisfaction, peaceful serenity, privileged security, and permanent success that is found through maintaining a right relationship with God.

Because the Lord is my shepherd

From the following verses, give phrases that identify the shepherd: Psalm 23:1; Genesis 48:15; 49:24; Hebrews 13:20; Revelation 7:17.

In Psalm 23:1, what personal pronouns are used? What do they imply?

If the shepherd guided, controlled, and cared for the sheep, he would in essence be their "lord." A paraphrase, therefore, would be, "The Lord is my Lord." Who is your lord? Who or what controls, shapes, and guides your life? The opinions of others? Your emotions? Or _____. (Fill in the blank.)

From Psalm 23:1, what is the obvious prerequisite for experiencing a lasting vacation?

Because the Lord is my supplier

When the Lord is your Lord, what promise can you claim from Psalm 23:1?

How does Isaiah 58:11 confirm this promise? What about Philippians 4:19?

What basic material, emotional, spiritual, or physical needs are you lacking?

What are two things we are encouraged to do in order to have our needs met? See Matthew 6:33; also compare Matthew 7:7 – 11 with 1 John 5:14 – 15.

From the following verses, how does God sometimes meet our needs? See Acts 20:34; Philippians 2:25; 2 Corinthians 9:12.

PEACEFUL SERENITY — Ps. 23:2 – 3

Through restoration

Reread Psalm 23:2 – 3. In what way does your soul need restoring? In what way do you need healing or mending on the inside?

Through rebirth

Why does your soul need restoring, according to Psalm 51:5; 38:18; 51:3; Romans 3:23; 6:23?

What is the first step to genuine serenity? See John 3:7; 1 John 1:9; Ephesians 1:7 – 8.

Through rest

What do you think the green pastures represent? Compare John 21:17 with John 6:35, 63.

What are some ways the shepherd "makes you lie down in green pastures"? How can this meet your inner needs?

Through refreshment

Drawing from your personal experience of being hot, tired, and thirsty, what does water mean to you?

What do the quiet waters represent in Psalm 23:2? See Jeremiah 2:13; John 4:10, 13 – 14; Revelation 7:17.

What are some of the ways that the shepherd leads you beside the quiet waters?

Through redirection

What path in life are you on? Consider the goals and priorities you have set as well as your desires.

According to Psalm 23:3, what is the implied wrong path? What is the right path?

At the end of your life, what difference will it make to be on the right path?

How does the reassurance that you are on the right path help you experience the serenity of a lasting vacation?

Ask the shepherd now to redirect you on the right path. Then, step out and follow Him.

PRIVILEGED SECURITY — Ps. 23:4

When facing death

What is the worst thing that could happen to you?

From Psalm 23:4, what makes the difference between terror and trust when the worst thing happens?

Give phrases from the following verses that underscore this difference: Isaiah 43:2; 63:9; Psalm 91:1 – 4.

When facing difficulties

What difficulties are you facing at home? At work? At church?

What comfort does Psalm 23:4 promise?

What do you think the "rod" represents, according to 2 Samuel 7:14; Job 9:34; Psalm 89:32; Proverbs 22:15?

How does this comfort you? See Proverbs 13:24; Hebrews 12:10 – 11.

What do you think the "staff" represents, according to Exodus 4:2, 4, 17; 14:16?

How does this comfort you? See Exodus 15:6; 2 Chronicles 20:6; Psalm 89:13; Jude 24 – 25.

PERMANENT SUCCESS — Ps. 23:5 – 6

What are some of the ways that a person's success is measured today? See Luke 12:16 – 21. How does this differ from success in God's eyes?

What are some of the keys to success from God's perspective, according to Joshua 1:7 – 8; Psalm 1; 2 Chronicles 20:20; Luke 12:29 – 31; Mark 8:36?

Relate each phrase of Psalm 23:5 – 6 to success in your own life.

Match each of the following references with one or more of the phrases in Psalm 23:5 – 6: 1 John 2:20, 27; 14:1 – 3; Psalm 5:12; 45:7; 133:1 – 3; 144:2; Hebrews 13:5 – 6; Revelation 19:6 – 9; 21:3; 22:3 – 5.

Isn't it time you enjoyed a "lasting vacation," based on the four main characteristics in Psalm 23? Start making plans for it today in order to begin experiencing genuine satisfaction, serenity, security, and success.

An Open Letter to the Weary

Thirty pastors' wives invited me to bring "Just Give Me Jesus," a revival for women, to the New Orleans Arena on the first anniversary of Hurricane Katrina. I accepted their invitation. Four days before the revival, I met with a group of local pastors and shared with them thoughts from the Old Testament prophet Haggai. His words were directed specifically to those who were weary of trying to rebuild the temple — God's house — when their own homes, along with everything else, lay in ruins. The book of Haggai has been preserved as an open letter to those who are weary of rebuilding and to those who have lost their passion for spiritual things.

Read Haggai 1:1 – 2:23

REORDER YOUR PRIORITIES

According to Haggai 1:1 – 6, what excuses did the people have for not rebuilding the temple?

What can the "temple" symbolize today? See 1 Corinthians 3:16 – 17; 6:19; Acts 11:26, 20:28; 1 Timothy 3:15.

To what are we to give first priority, according to Matthew 6:33; 8:18 – 22; 22:34 – 38?

What excuses do people give today for not making their relationship with God a priority?

What rebuke did God give the people in Haggai 1:5 – 11?

What similar rebukes did God give others in 1 Samuel 2:29 – 30; Malachi 1:6 – 11; Matthew 6:19 – 21; Luke 12:16 – 21; Mark 8:34 – 37?

How many times does the phrase "give careful thought" appear in the book of Haggai? List the verses.

Give careful thought to your ways now. Reflect on how you spend your money and time. What preoccupies your thoughts? What are your primary goals in life?

Could your weariness be due to misplaced priorities — trying to accomplish goals that are not God's? How will you reorder your private world to put His agenda first?

Close the door on the past

Read Haggai 2:1 – 3 and Ezra 3:10 – 13. On what were many of the older people focused? What painful comparison is robbing you of joy?

Read Isaiah 43:18; Ecclesiastes 3:15; Philippians 3:13 – 14. How do these verses encourage you?

Rewrite Matthew 6:22 – 23, substituting the word "focus" for "eye(s)." Explain these verses in terms of our perspective.

Matthew 6:24 describes someone who is "cross-eyed." To correct our vision, what should be our single focus? See 1 Corinthians 7:35; 2 Corinthians 11:3; Hebrews 12:2 – 3.

What is one practical way we can close the door on the past, reject painful comparisons, and refocus our perspective? See Nehemiah 1; Daniel 9:1 – 4.

List phrases from Psalm 27 that describe what we can do to stay focused. How will you incorporate these into your life?

Commit yourself in the present

What command did God give three times in Haggai 2:4? Give the modern equivalent of each group to whom the command was given. What other command did He give? What work has God given you to do?

What kind of strength is needed to overcome weariness in order to get back to work and complete the assignment?

What two promises did God give to encourage the weary workers? What similar encouragement do you receive from Joshua 1:6 – 9; 1 Chronicles 28:9 – 10, 20; Isaiah 40:27 – 31; 50:4; Jeremiah 31:25; Matthew 11:28; Galatians 6:9?

Open your eyes to Him

Read Haggai 2:9. What did God say to those who were so focused on the past that they were blinded to the future?

Read Malachi 3:1 and Matthew 21:12 – 14. In what specific way was the rebuilt temple more glorious than the original?

Read Ephesians 5:18; 2 Corinthians 3:18; 1 Peter 1:6 – 7; 1 John 3:2 – 3. How can your "temple" be more glorious tomorrow than today?

What is the ultimate glory that is our hope for the future? See Ephesians 1:18 – 21; John 17:24; Revelation 5:11 – 13; 15:1 – 4; 19:5 – 9.

REDIRECT YOUR PURPOSE

Read Haggai 2:10 – 12. How does the text show that righteousness is not contagious?

Read Genesis 6:8 – 9; 15:6; Psalm 35:28; and Philippians 3:9 with Romans 1:17; 10:17; 2 Timothy 3:16. How can we purposefully direct others toward God's righteousness?

Read Haggai 2:13 – 14. Give phrases that indicate sin is contagious. What can you do to stop sin from spreading in your life? Your family? Your city and country? The world?

In Haggai 2:15 – 19, how did God deal with Judah's sin?

How are these principles underscored by Deuteronomy 28:1 – 8, 15 – 25? How have you experienced the consequences of righteousness? Of sin?

How are these consequences motivating factors that help us to overcome weariness and to put God first?

What phrase in Haggai 2:10 – 23 reveals that God is the God of second chances? If your life is marred by sin and its consequences, how do you get a second chance from God? See Jeremiah 3:21 – 22; Acts 2:22 – 24, 36 – 38.

How does God give Peter a second chance in Mark 14:66 – 72; John 21:7 – 8, 15 – 22?

Would you thank God for giving you another chance by taking it? Redirect your life's purpose to live for His glory alone.

RECLAIM YOUR PRIVILEGE

What promise did God give to Zerubbabel in Haggai 2:20 – 22? What similar promise does He give to you and me? See Psalm 27:1 – 3; Proverbs 16:7; Isaiah 57:14 – 15.

What privileges did He give Zerubbabel in Haggai 2:23?

What similar privileges does He give us? See John 15:14 – 16; Romans 8:14 – 17; 1 John 3:1; 1 Thessalonians 1:4.

They finished building the temple according to the command of the God of Israel".[8]
When people look back on what you have done, what will be said of your life's work? That it remained unfinished because you became "weary of well doing"?[9] What will be said then is determined by what you do now. Don't let weariness waste your life or rob you of your eternal reward. Get back to work — now.

---

8. Ezra 6:14.
9. Galatians 6:9 KJV.

Guarding Against Burnout

In what way are you serving God inside or outside of your home? Have you ever been so emotionally spent, so spiritually depleted, so physically tired that you felt you could not continue in that service for one more moment? Even now, are you in danger of "burning out"?

Elijah is referred to more often in the New Testament than any other Old Testament prophet, and he appeared with Jesus on the Mount of Transfiguration. Malachi prophesied that Elijah would thunder onto the world scene immediately preceding the coming of Jesus Christ. Without question, Elijah was one of the greatest of the prophets, yet at one point in his service he suffered from burnout.

Read 1 Kings 17:1 – 10; 18:1 – 46; and 19:1 – 21

THE SIGNS OF BURNOUT

Spiritual intensity

From 1 Kings 17:1, what can be concluded about Elijah's occupation or position?

Intense service that was faithful to God

What evidence of Elijah's obedience do you find in 1 Kings 17:2 – 5; 17:8 – 10; 18:1 – 2?

What evidence of Elijah's dependence do you find in 1 Kings 18:30 – 37?

What evidence of Elijah's expectancy do you find in 1 Kings 18:41 – 45?

What evidence of obedience, dependence, and expectancy can be found in your service to God?

Intense service that was faulted by others

In 1 Kings 19:1 – 2, what was the official response of the leadership to Elijah's service?

How have others reacted and responded to your faithful service?

Emotional anxiety

List as many phrases as you can from 1 Kings 18 that reveal Elijah's courage.

What was his reaction to the criticism and faultfinding of others in 1 Kings 19:3?

What are you afraid of in service? How have you given in to your fears?

Personal self-pity

How did fear lead to faithlessness? Carefully read 1 Kings 19:4.

What do you think were some of Elijah's thoughts that caused him to feel that his service to God was not worth the risk?

Have you ever considered resigning from ministry? Why?

In what way are you so discouraged that you have lapsed into self-pity?

THE SOLUTIONS TO BURNOUT

What solutions have you sought for burnout? Ask God to open your heart to receive the following solutions.

Practical

What was the very first thing God did to encourage His worn-out, burned-out servant in 1 Kings 19:5 – 6?

What was the second thing?

The third thing?

How can you apply this to your situation?

What do you learn from the way God dealt with Elijah?

Supernatural

In 1 Kings 19:5, 7, what did God do for Elijah that was beyond human ability?

When have you asked God for a fresh touch of His Spirit in your life?

Do you think Elijah could have recovered without the fresh touch from God?

Spiritual

From Elijah's answer in 1 Kings 19:10, what do you think God was seeking to do by asking the question in verse 9?

In 1 Kings 19:11 – 12, what two attributes of His nature did God dramatize to help Elijah overcome his fears?

God repeated His question of 1 Kings 19:9 in 1 Kings 19:13. What was God trying to get Elijah to confront?

How did God's answer in 1 Kings 19:15 – 18 help Elijah to overcome his faithlessness?

What do you do and to whom do you go for spiritual encouragement?

Personal

Recalled

What did God tell Elijah to do in 1 Kings 19:15 – 16?

From 1 Kings 19:17 – 18, how did God, even in His recall of Elijah, continue to encourage him?

Did God give Elijah any assurance that he would not be criticized or threatened again — that this time his service would be easier? Reflect on your answer.

How would this give Elijah a deep conviction of his calling to serve?

Have you ever felt burned out? How did you handle it? What do you think would happen if you asked God to recall you into service?

Recommitted

From 1 Kings 19:19, how long did Elijah apparently wait before answering God's call?

How prompt are you in carrying out what God has called you to do?

Reinforced

How did God provide for Elijah's reinforcement in 1 Kings 19:16?

When Jesus sent out His disciples, what is implied by the way their names are listed in Matthew 10:2 – 4?

What visible person has God provided to reinforce you in service?

What invisible person has He provided for you, according to John 14:15 – 17?

Will you ask God to provide you with an earthly, visible companion in service?

Will you be willing to be that reinforcement to someone else in service — a spouse, a pastor, or a Sunday school teacher?

Would you open your heart to receive God's solutions and make yourself available to be recalled into service? Don't burn out. Burn on!

Well Rested

Have you ever been examined by a doctor who told you, "There is nothing wrong with you. You just need a rest"?

In your fast-paced, stressed-out life, do you lack rest? Do you actually long for it? I do. There have been times when even a hospital stay has appeared attractive simply because of the rest it would seem to afford.

There is hope. It's summertime, when traditionally the living should be easy — when life should kick back, shift gears, and go at a more leisurely pace. It's a time when many take a vacation. But in my life, the only difference summer seems to make in my overloaded schedule is that it's hot outside.

So as summer turns into fall, I find myself looking over my shoulder wistfully, longing for the rest I haven't had. I want to be really rested. Well rested. I need the kind of rest only God can give … the rest that the writer to the Hebrews described as being something of a trilogy, with three distinct parts.

Read Hebrews 4:1 – 11

PHYSICAL REST

The example of physical rest

Give a phrase from Hebrews 4:1 – 11 that refers to physical rest.

Describe this physical rest from Genesis 2:1 – 3.

Did God intend for His example to be a pattern for our lives? See Isaiah 58:13 – 14. What benefits result from the principle of setting aside one day in seven for physical rest and spiritual refocusing? Put them in your own words. How closely do you follow God's example?

Give phrases from the following verses that underscore this principle: Exodus 16:23; 23:12; 34:21; Leviticus 23:3.

Give the phrase from Leviticus 16:31 that indicates that this principle transcends time and is in effect today.

Make a list of what you are doing on Sunday that can be done Monday through Saturday. Some examples are shopping, housework, laundry, yard work, business calls, travel, and email. Transfer these activities to another day of the week and reserve Sunday for physical rest and spiritual refreshment.

The experience of physical rest

The ark of the covenant that led the children of Israel through the wilderness signified God in their midst. Keeping this in mind, what do you learn from Numbers 10:33?

Give phrases from the following verses that reveal God's intention for physical rest to be not only a theory but an experience: Joshua 1:13; 21:44; 1 Kings 8:56; 2 Chronicles 14:6; Psalm 23:1 – 2; Jeremiah 31:2; Mark 6:31.

How much time have you made for physical rest during the past week, the past month, the past year?

Are you physically exhausted because you're working 24/7 and not following God's example? If so, what are you going to do about it?

What will you do to build times of physical rest into your life so that it is not just a longing or a need but an actual experience?

It's possible to go on the most relaxing, refreshing vacation we've ever experienced, yet return only partially rested because, although our bodies are relaxed, our spirits are weary. We need spiritual rest.

SPIRITUAL REST

How does Proverbs 6:9 – 11 indicate that physical rest alone is insufficient and can actually be detrimental if not balanced with hard work?

Give phrases from Hebrews 4:1 – 11 that refer to spiritual rest.

How is spiritual rest related to physical rest? See Psalm 4:8.

What other words for spiritual rest can you think of? See John 14:27; Philippians 4:11 – 12; Jeremiah 31:25.

What are some things we must do to experience spiritual rest? See Philippians 4:6 – 9; Psalm 119:165.

From each of the following verses, describe one aspect of spiritual rest: Exodus 33:14; Deuteronomy 12:10; 33:12; 2 Chronicles 15:15; Psalm 62:5; 91:1; 116:7; Proverbs 19:23; Jeremiah 6:16; Matthew 11:28 – 29.

A lack of physical rest can make us tired and irritable. Give characteristics of the lack of spiritual rest from Jeremiah 45:1 – 5; Habakkuk 2:4 – 5; Isaiah 57:20 – 21; Ecclesiastes 2:23; 5:10.

What is the primary reason you and I don't enter into spiritual rest? See Hebrews 3:19.

What can you do to avoid being spiritually weary even though you are physically rested? See 1 Peter 3:8 – 12.

How much of an effort are you making "to enter that rest"? See Hebrews 4:11.

The nineteenth-century Scottish evangelist Henry Drummond said that rest "is not a hallowed feeling that comes over us in church. It is … the repose of a heart set deep in God." Do you need spiritual rest? Rest from the self-effort of trying to please God? Rest from plotting revenge? Rest from manipulating people or circumstances to get your way? Rest from worry, fear, anger, or self-pity? Are you wearily wandering in the wilderness of self-reliance instead of totally surrendering to the authority of Christ — where you can enter the promised land of God's full blessing and rest in Him alone?

One day all of our burdens will be laid down and all of our strivings will cease — when we enter into eternal rest.

ETERNAL REST

Give phrases from Hebrews 4:1 – 11 that refer to eternal rest.

How do the following verses also point to eternal rest: Job 3:17; Isaiah 57:2; Revelation 14:13?

From Revelation 21:3 – 5, list some of the characteristics of eternal rest. Put each of them in your own words.

What phrase from Hebrews 4:1 – 11 indicates that you will not be truly well rested until you enter your heavenly home?

Before summer ends, take time and make the decision to be well rested. Follow God's example by building into your schedule a time for physical rest and refreshment. Reexamine the conditions for spiritual rest and make sure you meet each one. Then relax and look forward to going to your Father's house, where you will be truly rested — forever.

September

INVOLVEMENT

Changing the World

When you watch the evening news on television or read your morning newspaper, do you ever react by desperately wishing you could change the decisions and discussions and debates — or the attitudes and actions and aims — into those which would truly benefit others and glorify God? Do you ever yearn for the world to be changed into a place where God's will is done here on earth as it is in heaven? Do you become so discouraged at the overwhelming odds against that kind of change that you shrug, sigh, and become even more immersed in your own affairs? Before you give up altogether, consider this: Maybe the world can be changed after all ... one person at a time.

The first chapter in the Bible gives you and me the keys to changing our world.

Read Genesis 1

THE DESPERATE CONDITION

From Genesis 1:2, give four descriptive words or phrases of planet Earth.

How could each description apply to the condition of a human life?

Who do you know who fits this description? How likely is that person going to change on their own?

THE DELIBERATE PREPARATION

From Genesis 1:1 – 3, what catalyst did God use to prepare the earth for change?

Give other examples of change brought about by this same catalyst from John 16:5 – 15; Romans 8:1 – 5, 11, 14 – 16; and from comparing John 18:17, 25 – 27 with Acts 4:8, 20.

What can you do to activate this catalyst in the life of the person you identified above? See Mark 9:17 – 19, 28 – 29; James 5:13 – 18; 1 Peter 4:7.

When and how will you work to deliberately prepare the person for change?

Who do you know who has been changed as a result of this type of preparation?

Who do you know will likely not be changed because of the lack of this type of preparation?

THE DAILY TRANSFORMATION

From Genesis 1:3 – 31, how many times does the phrase "and God said" (or the equivalent) occur? List the verses.

How many times does the phrase "and it was so" (or the equivalent) occur? List the verses.

Does the first phrase "and God said" ever occur without the second phrase "and it was so" (or equivalents)? What foundational principle does this teach you?

How is this foundational principle confirmed in Psalm 119:89? In Matthew 5:18; 24:35; 2 Timothy 3:16; 2 Peter 1:20 – 21; Revelation 22:6?

List the changes, with the corresponding verses, that took place in response to God's Word.

Apply each change in the process of creation to that which takes place in a human life in response to the power of God's Spirit and God's Word. (Example: In verse 3, God's Word brought light into the darkness. God's Word brings the light of truth, understanding, and faith into the darkness of falsity, ignorance, and unbelief.)

Did all of these changes take place at one time? If not, how did they occur?

Although the changes were different, what factors were consistently the same each day?

Are these same factors present in your life? What can you do to help establish them in the life of the person you identified?

Contrast Genesis 1:2 with Genesis 1:28 – 31. What are some of the most striking results of the changes that were made?

What does it mean to you to be created by God? To be created in God's image? To be created male or female?

What do you need to do so that God can change you into a person in whom He can see His own image reflected? See 2 Corinthians 3:18; 1 Peter 1:6 – 7.

What changes need to take place in your life for the Creator to say it is "very good"?

If, in the beginning, God could transform planet Earth from a place in desperate condition to a place where He could see His own reflection, there is no reason He can't bring about change today, starting with your own life and that of your loved one.

Change We Can Believe In

During America's presidential elections, the theme of "change" echoes in one form or another, from one campaign to another. The idea of change strikes a chord that resonates with young and old, rich and poor, men and women, black and white and brown. Thinking of this recurring need for change, I began to wonder: Is the change that people long for, and politicians promise, a change that can truly be delivered? Or are people who are seeking change confusing the political and the spiritual? Are they looking for something that only God can give?

The older I get, the more I want things to be familiar. I find myself choosing the same restaurants to frequent, the same clothing styles to wear, the same friends to enjoy, the same exercise patterns to follow, even the same place to sit in church. Change can be unsettling; it requires energy that taxes my strength and mental reserves. So I don't want change just for the sake of change. I want change that is worthwhile, change I can really believe in.

The good news is that we can always believe in the change God is bringing. And remember this: "God chooses the foolish things of this world to shame the wise, the weak to shame the strong."[10] Not one of us is too small to make a difference.

---

10. 1 Corinthians 1:27.

CHANGE FOR SINNERS

Give at least four or five phrases from Ephesians 2:1 – 3 that describe sinners.

What is the sinner's condition as described in Romans 1:18; John 3:36?

According to Ephesians 2:4, who took the initiative to change our sinful condition?

Copy Ephesians 2:4 – 5, substituting your name for the personal pronouns.

Read Ephesians 2:6 – 7. List phrases that reveal the dramatic change in a sinner's condition. Contrast these with phrases from Ephesians 2:1 – 3.

Read Ephesians 2:8 – 9. State what is necessary in order to truly change.

Read Ephesians 1:11 – 12 and 2:10. What is one purpose for the changes described in this passage? Do you think politics or government can truly change sinners, from God's perspective? Explain your reasoning based on these verses.

CHANGE OF STATUS

Who were the Gentiles in Ephesians 2:11? Who do they represent today?

Read Ephesians 2:11 – 12. List three phrases that describe our spiritual status.

Read Ephesians 2:12. Because of our original status, what was our spiritual condition?

Read Ephesians 2:12 – 13 and John 5:24. What dramatic change is described in Ephesians 2:13? Who brought it about? How was it accomplished?

How is this change in status referred to in John 1:12 and 15:15? In Romans 8:17? In Galatians 3:29 and 4:7? Ephesians 3:6 and 2:19? 1 Peter 2:10? Acts 26:18?

What is one result of this change, repeatedly referred to in Ephesians 2:14 – 15, 17? Describe that result in your own words.

Do you think peace in the human heart can be achieved through politics or legislation? Explain your answer.

CHANGE FOR SHATTERED LIVES

List the kind of lives that are shattered, according to 1 Corinthians 6:9 – 10.

Are these shattered lives hopeless and incapable of change? See 1 Corinthians 6:11.

What dramatic change in shattered lives is referred to in Ephesians 2:20?

If our lives are like a building, who is the foundation and how do we lay it? See Ephesians 2:20; 1 Corinthians 3:11.

What is a cornerstone and why is it important? (Refer to a dictionary.)

In the analogy of our lives, who is the cornerstone, according to Ephesians 2:20; Acts 4:11; 1 Peter 2:6 – 7?

What or who are the building blocks? See 1 Peter 2:5.

Read Ephesians 2:21 – 22. Describe the before and the ultimate after of a shattered life changed through the power of the cross.

Whom do you know who desperately needs change? I am convinced that the real change we all long for is one that takes place in individual lives, from the inside out, beginning with a change of heart and mind. Such change can only be found in a personal relationship with the Lord Jesus Christ and the indwelling of His Holy Spirit. Will you recommit to telling others about change we can believe in, change through faith in Jesus Christ and through the power of His cross? Then be a living demonstration of it.

Getting Serious

After a recent speaking engagement, I was interviewed by a journalist from a leading Christian publication. The journalist was fascinated not just by the message I had given, but by the way I had given it. He indicated that none of the popular Bible teachers and speakers had such a confronting, in-your-face presentation style. Instead, he said, the trend was going more to the suggestive, thoughtful delivery. He said the best speakers were getting away from the authoritative and confronting style of preaching. Then he asked me why I spoke in the style that I did.

I never preplan how I deliver a message. After prayerfully preparing it, I just release it. As I have reflected on the journalist's question, I know the way the message is "released" comes from my heart and the deep inner conviction of truth that is there. It also comes from the very serious way I take my service to Christ.

I am convinced that the time to serve Christ is now! The words of Jesus haunt me continuously, "As long as it is day, we must do the work of him who sent me. Night is coming, when no one can work."[11] Time is running out. The night is coming. It's time to get serious about our service to Christ.

---

11. John 9:4.

Read 2 Timothy 4

GET SERIOUS ABOUT THE CHARGE — 2 Tim. 4:1 – 5

Give the three descriptive phrases in 2 Timothy 4:1 that set up the charge. Match each phrase with one of the following verses: John 14:17 – 18, 20, 23; 1 Corinthians 3:12 – 16; 2 Peter 3:10 – 12; Matthew 24:42, 44 – 46.

Describe the seriousness implied by each phrase. Apply each phrase to your own situation.

Be prepared

According to 1 Corinthians 3:1 – 2; 2 Timothy 2:15, 20 – 21; Titus 3:1; 1 Peter 3:15; Ephesians 5:15 – 17, what are some ways to be prepared?

Read 2 Timothy 4:2. What do you think Paul meant when he instructed Timothy to "be prepared in season and out of season"? How prepared are you?

Be patient

From 2 Timothy 4:2 – 3, why do you think patience is required of those who are serious about their service?

Why is this same patience necessary for the sower in the parable of Matthew 13:1 – 9, 18 – 23?

How does James 5:7 – 8 emphasize this kind of patience?

Be perseverant

List the phrases in 2 Timothy 4:5. Explain what is meant by each phrase using the following verses: Titus 2:12; 1 Peter 1:13; 4:7; 2 Peter 1:5 – 8; 2 Timothy 2:3 – 7; Mark 16:15; Acts 1:8; 4:20.

Have you ever quit before finishing a job? A responsibility? A commitment? Explain.

What can you do to increase your perseverance? See Galatians 6:7 – 9; Hebrews 12:1 – 3.

How serious are you about the charge? Serious enough to take it to heart?

GET SERIOUS ABOUT THE CROWN — 2 Tim. 4:6 – 8

Name the crowns that are promised to God's children and what they are rewarded for. Read 1 Corinthians 9:24 – 27; 1 Thessalonians 2:19; 2 Timothy 4:8; James 1:12; Revelation 2:10; 1 Peter 5:2 – 4.

Do you think it's possible to be saved and get into heaven, yet not have a crown? Explain. See 1 Corinthians 3:11 – 15; Revelation 3:11.

What do you think we may do with the crowns when we receive them? See Revelation 4:9 – 11.

Five minutes before you see Jesus face-to-face, what regrets will you have? Will you wish you had been serious about the crown? Will you get serious now ... before night comes?

GET SERIOUS ABOUT THE COST — 2 Tim. 4:9 – 22

The personal cost

What personal price did Paul pay for taking seriously his service to Christ? See 2 Timothy 4:10.

How did Jesus also pay this same price for doing His Father's will? See Mark 14:50 – 52.

Have you been deserted by your friends for doing the right thing? How are you encouraged by Hebrews 13:5 – 6?

The spiritual cost

What spiritual price did Paul pay at the end of his faithful, fruitful life? See 2 Timothy 4:14 – 15.

Read Matthew 4:1; 1 Peter 5:8 – 9; Ephesians 6:10 – 11. Are the servants of God ever exempt from this "cost"?

Has someone been attacking you? How should you respond? See Matthew 5:11 – 12, 43 – 48; 1 Peter 4:19.

The emotional cost

What emotional price did Paul pay for staying focused on God's will for his life? See 2 Timothy 4:9, 16, 21.

If you are lonely, how do the following verses encourage you: Psalm 23:4; Isaiah 43:1 – 4; Psalm 91:14 – 16?

The material cost

What material things did Paul lack? See 2 Timothy 4:13.

From a New Testament perspective, do you think illness, poverty, and problems are a sign of God's disfavor? Answer with a phrase from each of the following verses: Philippians 1:12 – 14; 2 Timothy 1:11 – 12; Revelation 1:9; 1 Peter 3:13 – 14; Matthew 8:20; Mark 15:24.

What material things do you lack? Is this evidence that God doesn't love you? That He isn't blessing you? That you've made a wrong choice? What could be His reason for allowing you to be in this situation? See 2 Corinthians 12:7 – 10; 1 Peter 1:6 – 7.

The ultimate cost

Paul gave everything, including his own life, in order to serve Christ. Read 2 Timothy 4:17 – 18 and name at least five things Paul received for the price he paid.

Do you think Paul had any regrets for taking his service to Christ so seriously? Why or why not?

Besides Paul, who is our example in giving everything in order to receive all that God has? See Hebrews 12:1 – 3.

Second Timothy is the last letter Paul ever wrote. As far as we know, he never saw Timothy again. Instead, within a relatively few short months of putting down his pen, church tradition says he was dragged outside of the city, where the Roman soldiers chopped off his head.

I can almost hear Paul's voice raised in the chorus of Revelation 5:12 – 13: "Worthy is the Lamb that was slain." Can you sing it now, not just by the words you say, but by the life you live and the service you give?

God doesn't want careless, casual Christians in His service. In the Old Testament, He whittled down Gideon's army from 32,000 men to 300 by cutting out those who did not take service to Him more seriously than anything else. In God's army today, would you make the cut?

It's time to get serious!

Exactly how are we to be the salt of the earth[12] that Jesus said His disciples would be? I have found that often a powerful impact on the world is preceded by a time of isolation and separation. For example:

+ Joseph was separated from the world when he was enslaved and imprisoned for more than thirteen years before he was then sent into the world as Egypt's second-in-command. As a result, his own family, as well as all of Egypt, benefited during years of famine and hardship.
+ Moses was separated from the world in a remote part of the desert for forty years before being sent into the world as the deliverer of the Hebrew people. As a result, an entire nation was set free from slavery and molded into the people of God.
+ Elijah was separated from the world for three years beside the brook Cherith, then at the widow's home in Zarephath, before being sent into the world to confront King Ahab and the priests of Baal on Mount Carmel. As a result, the entire northern kingdom of Israel witnessed a historic, unprecedented display of God's power.

---

12. See Matthew 5:13 – 15.

- Jesus Himself was separated from the world for thirty years as a carpenter in Nazareth before being sent into the world for public ministry. The result was the redemption of the human race, forgiveness of sin, and heaven opened for you and me.

This pattern of separation before service is clearly illustrated in the life of Abraham.

Read Genesis 12:1 – 15:1

SEPARATED FOR GOD'S PERSPECTIVE

In worship

What pattern did Abraham establish early in his life of faith? List phrases from Genesis 12:7 – 8; 13:4.

How do the following verses confirm the necessity of this pattern for our lives if we are to have God's perspective? See 1 Chronicles 16:11, 34 – 35; 2 Chronicles 18:3 – 4; Psalm 119:45 – 47; Proverbs 9:10; 28:5; Hebrews 11:6.

How does the Bible describe those who do not seek God? Read Psalm 10:4; 14:1 – 4.

How can we understand God's perspective if we don't spend time with Him?

In watching

As Abraham spent time with the Lord, he also watched the world.

Describe Abraham's relationship with God in Genesis 13:14 – 18.

What did Abraham see happening in the world around him in Genesis 14:1 – 12?

What is happening in the world around you? List changes, problems, and tensions you see.

What do you think Jesus meant in John 18:36?

How does 2 Chronicles 7:14 underscore that Jesus' kingdom is His reign in the hearts of people?

How do you think God might have you in "seclusion" so you can spend time with Him in worship while you watch the world around you?

How does this change your perspective?

How might God be preparing to send you into the world to rescue people who are held captive by the enemy?

SEPARATED TO RELY ON GOD'S POWER

Recognizing His call

What did God use to call Abraham out of seclusion and into active involvement? See Genesis 14:12 – 14.

How was Abraham's involvement a godly response? Reflect on John 3:16.

In what ways have problems and changes in our world affected you or a loved one personally?

How might these issues be God's call to get you involved in that particular sphere?

How was Nehemiah's call similar in Nehemiah 1:1 – 2:6?

Will you ask God to open your eyes to His call to serve?

Rescuing the captives

How did Abraham respond to the news of his nephew's capture by the enemy? See Genesis 14:14 – 17.

Who is the enemy of the child of God? See 1 Peter 5:8; Ephesians 6:11 – 12; Luke 8:12; John 8:44; 1 John 3:8; Revelation 2:10; 12:9; 20:10.

What are some of the things the enemy uses today to hold people captive?

What loved one of yours has been taken captive by the enemy? How have you responded?

What resources did Abraham have to fight the enemy? List phrases from Genesis 14:13 – 14.

What are your resources for fighting the enemy? See John 15:5; 8:32; Ephesians 6:17 – 20; 2 Corinthians 10:3 – 4; 3:17.

What encouragement do you receive from the following Scriptures? See Zechariah 4:6; 1 Samuel 17:45 – 47; 1 John 4:4; 2 Chronicles 20:15; 1 John 5:5; 2 Corinthians 10:3 – 4; Philippians 4:13.

Using a map, estimate how far Abraham went in pursuit of the captives from Hebron to Hobah, north of Damascus. Describe the effort required for such a pursuit. What was the result? See Genesis 14:16.

How far are you willing to go to pursue the enemy and set the captives free? Compare your effort to the effort of the Christians in Acts 12:5 – 17; Colossians 4:2, 12.

Who benefited from Abraham's involvement? See Genesis 14:16 – 24. Who will benefit from your involvement?

What would be the effect on our world if, instead of reacting to our circumstances by complaining, wringing our hands, or blaming and criticizing others, we separated ourselves to God in worship while we watched the world around us? And then, as we gained God's perspective and recognized His call to serve, we relied not on programs or techniques but on His power as we pursue those who are being held captive by the enemy? Let's find out.

Get Ready to Step Out

During the time that I began holding "Just Give Me Jesus" arena revivals for women, I meditated on the book of Joshua in my personal devotions. Morning after morning, God seemed to speak to me through Joshua's experiences and his testimony, instructing me in how to get ready for the challenge of holding the revivals.

As I share with you some of the principles God taught me, I wonder if you are also facing a challenge in service to Him. Maybe He has challenged you ...

to walk across the street to share the gospel with a neighbor.

to open up His Word for a Sunday school class.

to live out your faith in Christ at your workplace.

to give your child the freedom to go to the foreign mission field.

to plant a church or inner-city ministry.

to visit those in prison or in hospitals or rest homes.

I've learned that an incredibly rich dimension of knowing God is reserved for those who step out of their comfort zones and walk by faith. Has God challenged you to step out of your comfort zone?

If not, get ready.

Read Joshua 1, 2, and 6

The Israelites had wandered for forty years in the wilderness, going nowhere with God. Then God instructed them, under Joshua's leadership, to get ready to step out of where they had been and into all that He wanted to give them. The challenge God issued to the entire nation of Israel became very personal to Joshua. Since his youth, he had been Moses' personal aide. He knew that God had appointed him as Moses' successor. When Moses died, it was time for Joshua to step out of his comfort zone.

OPEN YOUR EARS TO GOD'S WORD — Josh. 1:1 – 9

Open your ears readily

Describe the possible impact of Moses' death on Joshua — emotionally, spiritually, practically, and professionally.

How could this impact have affected Joshua's readiness to listen to the voice of God?

When your life is in turmoil, how ready are you to read your Bible and to listen to God?

Open your ears respectfully

From Joshua's experience as a slave in Egypt and during the Exodus, what did he know about God? See Exodus 12:1 – 3, 12 – 13, 29 – 31; 14:9 – 28; 15:1 – 3. Then see Exodus 17:8 – 16; 19:18 – 19; 24:13 – 18; 33:7, 11. Finally, see Numbers 27:18 – 23.

What difference do you think Joshua's knowledge of God made in the way he listened to God?

What do you know about the Lord from your own experience and from Scripture? How does that knowledge affect the way you listen to Him?

Open your ears receptively

What command is repeated three times in Joshua 1:6 – 9? Apply it to what God has told you to do.

List the other commands given in Joshua 1:6 – 9. Give a personal application for each.

List the promises in Joshua 1:3 – 9. Which one is most meaningful to you?

Which promise would be most meaningful to someone getting ready to step out in faith?

OPEN YOUR LIFE TO GOD'S WILL — Josh. 1:10 – 18

It was God's will for Joshua that he step out in faith, leading His people out of where they were and into the place God wanted them to be.

From Joshua 1:10 – 15, give evidence of Joshua's obedience to God and his confidence in God.

How was Joshua encouraged in Joshua 1:16 – 18?

What phrase indicates that God was speaking through the people to reassure Joshua? See Joshua 1:16 – 18.

Whom has God used to reassure you as you step out of your comfort zone?

OPEN YOUR EYES TO GOD'S WORLD — Josh. 2 and 6

As Joshua got ready to step out of where he was and into the place God wanted him to be, he kept his eyes open to the world around him.

Why do you think Joshua sent two spies to look over the land in Joshua 2:1?

Did the information they brought back help Joshua defeat Jericho? See Joshua 6:1 – 5.

What reason could God have had for sending spies to Jericho? See Joshua 2:1 – 21.

What similarities can you find between the story of Rahab (Joshua 2:1 – 21; 6:22 – 25) and the Samaritan woman (John 4:4 – 30)? What differences?

What does this knowledge teach you about God's love for the world as He leads you into new territory? About His love for individuals?

As you look at the world around you, what need has come to your attention? What opportunity has been presented to you for involvement?

Skim Joshua 3 – 6. Make a list of things that would not have taken place if Joshua had been unwilling to open his ears, his eyes, and his life to God.

What was the result of Joshua's openness to God? What difference will your openness to God make — in your own life and in the world around you? Will you get ready to step out of your comfort zone by opening yourself up to God? Someone's salvation may depend on it.

October

TIME

Defeating the Greatest Enemy

We can't help but notice the evil around us. We often feel targeted as individuals and as a nation by hate-filled enemies. Our newspapers, magazines, and television talk shows fill us with information about specific villains and how to protect ourselves from them. From time to time, the entire nation is put on high alert as warnings of imminent danger are issued. Our military and intelligence agencies are operating offensively twenty-four hours a day around the world.

Although the global networks of terrorists pose a real and present danger, Christians have an even more deadly enemy — the Devil — who is dedicated to our utter destruction. And God has put us on high alert, warning us of the daily danger of attack that we face. He also has given us instructions not only on how to defend ourselves but also on how to seize the offensive in order to have victory.

Only when we have learned how to confront our unseen enemy will we be equipped to deal with the evil we see in the world around us.

To the opponent

Who is our enemy? Give his names from Genesis 3:4; Matthew 4:3; 12:24; 13:19; John 8:44; 14:30; 2 Corinthians 4:4; 11:14; Ephesians 2:2; 6:16; 1 Peter 5:8; Revelation 12:10.

What do his names reveal about his character? His purpose? If necessary, use a dictionary to define his names.

To the opposition

What word in Ephesians 6:12 indicates that it is not easy to defeat the Devil?

Is the opposition always obvious? Give your reasons from Ephesians 6:12; 2 Corinthians 11:14.

What are two of the Devil's oldest and most effective schemes? Compare Matthew 3:17 with Matthew 4:3. What was the Devil doing? What was he inferring? Put his statement from Matthew 4:3 into your own words.

How was his attack on Eve in Genesis 3:1 similar?

What tactic of the Devil do you see in Ephesians 6:16?

What flaming arrows has he hurled your way?

Describe in everyday terms how the Devil attacks in relationships.

Compare Job 1:1 – 11 with Zechariah 3:1. See also Revelation 12:10.

BE ASSURED

When going against the Devil, what assurance does the believer have? Give phrases from Ephesians 1:19 – 23; 6:10; Hebrews 2:14 – 15; 1 John 4:4; 5:5; Revelation 12:10 – 11.

What future does the Devil face, according to Romans 16:20; Revelation 20:10?

BE ARMED

What is one thing that makes us vulnerable to the Devil's attack, according to Ephesians 4:26 – 27?

How do we defeat the Devil, according to Ephesians 6:13; James 4:7; 1 Peter 5:8?

How did Jesus defeat the Devil in Matthew 4:1 – 11?

What are some of the reasons why Eve did not defeat him in Genesis 3:1 – 6?

How many pieces of armor are listed in Ephesians 6:13 – 18? Describe the practical and spiritual use of each piece.

How much of the armor protects the back of the warrior? What does this tell you about our position toward the Devil?

Which pieces are for defense? Which ones are for offense?

Which pieces are you missing?

Write how you will apply and implement each piece in your life today.

What difficulty are you experiencing in your health? Your relationships? Your job? Your finances? Your school or church or family or ministry? Could the difficulty be opposition from the Devil? In what way are you being tempted physically? Financially? Socially? Professionally?

Instead of being defeated by the difficulty or yielding to the temptation, choose to be alert, assured, and armed. Don't live just somehow. Live triumphantly!

A Wake-Up Call

Have you ever slept through your alarm — or found out, too late, that it didn't go off because you had set it for p.m. instead of a.m.?

When I'm traveling, I have learned that I need actual wake-up calls! And from time to time, I also need spiritual wake-up calls. The daily routine of responsibilities, the never-ending challenge of deadlines, the persistent pressure of problems, and the hectic pace of life tend to preoccupy my thoughts and time with the urgency of the moment. If I'm not careful, I may miss something vitally important that God has for me — something He may want me to see or do — some blessing He wants to give me or wants me to pass along to someone else.

And so He gives me a wake-up call. The call is usually disguised as a crisis in my life or in my spirit that plunges me to my knees, where He opens my eyes.

Read Isaiah 6:1 – 8

OPEN YOUR EYES

Describe the wake-up call that opened Isaiah's eyes in Isaiah 6:1. How do you think Isaiah was affected by Uzziah's death emotionally? Spiritually?

When Isaiah opened his eyes, who or what specifically did he see? Compare Isaiah 6:1, 4 with John 12:41.

Put into your own words each phrase that describes the Lord in Isaiah 6:1 – 3.

Match a phrase from Isaiah 6:1 – 3 with the following verses: Ezekiel 1:25 – 28; Revelation 4:2, 8; 5:13; Genesis 14:19 – 20; Numbers 24:16; Job 22:12; 1 Chronicles 29:11; Exodus 15:1; Acts 5:31; Ephesians 4:8; 1 Peter 1:15 – 16.

Do you think Isaiah would have opened his eyes if he had not had the wake-up call?

What has God allowed in your life that could be His wake-up call to you? What difference has it made in your life?

Give the main points of Isaiah's sermon from Isaiah 5:8, 11, 18, 20 – 22. To whom was he speaking?

How is Isaiah's own response to seeing the Lord similar in Isaiah 6:5 to his repeated condemnation of others in 5:8 – 22? How is it different?

Give phrases from the following verses that indicate a response similar to Isaiah's: Job 42:5 – 6; Luke 5:4 – 8; Revelation 1:17; Ephesians 5:13 – 14.

How is this response affirmed in Psalm 51:17; Isaiah 57:15; 2 Corinthians 7:8 – 11; Revelation 3:19?

What do you think is meant by rending your heart? Is it an option? See Joel 2:12 – 13; Matthew 4:17; Luke 13:3; Acts 3:19.

Use the following references to pinpoint sin that you need to repent of in your own life: Romans 1:21; Hebrews 3:19; Matthew 23:28; 1 John 2:16; 1 Timothy 5:8; 1 Corinthians 3:3; Malachi 3:8.

Is anyone exempt from the need to repent? See James 2:10; 4:17; Romans 3:10, 23; 2 Peter 3:9.

When was the last time that you wept in grief over your own sin?

RETURN TO THE CROSS

Since a burning coal applied to the lips would be very painful, what could this represent? See John 16:8; Hebrews 12:11; Psalm 32:3 – 5.

What did the altar illustrate in Isaiah 6:6? See Romans 3:24 – 25; Hebrews 9:14, 22; 1 John 1:9.

What hope does God offer ruined sinners like Isaiah? See Isaiah 1:18. To sinners like you and me? See Acts 10:43; 26:18; Ephesians 1:7; Colossians 1:13 – 14; Romans 8:1.

What is hindering you from returning to the cross and repenting of your sin? Do it now.

JUST SAY YES

What was the connection between Isaiah's repentance and his experience in Isaiah 6:8?

Read Isaiah 6:8; Nehemiah 1:1 – 11; Exodus 3:1 – 10; Luke 5:4 – 11; John 21:16 – 19; Acts 9:1 – 6; 13:2. How were these calls of God the same? How were they different?

What is your calling, according to the following Scriptures: Romans 1:6; 8:28 – 30; 1 Corinthians 1:2, 9; 7:15; Galatians 5:13; Philippians 3:14; Colossians 3:15; 1 Timothy 6:12; 2 Timothy 1:9; 1 Peter 2:9, 20 – 21; 3:9; Revelation 1:5 – 6; 17:14; John 21:19 – 22?

How does your response to God's call compare with Isaiah's in Isaiah 6:8? Simon Peter's in Luke 5:10 – 11? Matthew's (or Levi's) in Luke 5:27 – 28?

Isaiah responded to God's wake-up call by opening his eyes, rending his heart, and committing his life to serve God. He went on to become the greatest of the Old Testament prophets.

Do you yearn for a life of significance? Do you long to make a difference in your world? Is your heart broken for those who are stepping into eternity ... lost forever? Are you grieved for the church that has a "form of godliness" but denies God's power?

Then this is your wake-up call. Open your eyes! Rend your heart! Return to the cross! Say yes to God.

Spiritual Day-Timers

Do you use a calendar arranged by the hours in each day, the days in each week, the weeks in each month, and the months in each year? I use one to quickly reference my schedule so that I don't forget something I'm supposed to be doing or a place I'm supposed to be. I used to have my schedule in a little black notebook. Then I upgraded to a PDA, an electronic organizer. Now my schedule can be accessed on a cell phone.

Jesus said that you and I are to be spiritual "day-timers." We are to be consciously aware of the day — the opportunities God gives us each hour, day, week, month, and year to do His work — and take those opportunities!

Read John 9:1 – 7

SEE THE OPPORTUNITY

In everyday life — John 9:1

What was Jesus doing when He saw the blind man?

What was Jesus doing when He called His first disciples in Mark 1:16 – 18? When He taught eternal truths in Mark 10:17 – 31? When He healed Bartimaeus in Mark 10:46 – 52?

What were Peter and John doing when they healed the crippled beggar in Acts 3:1 – 8? What was Paul doing when he witnessed to the Athenian intellectuals in Acts 17:15 – 17?

What do each of these examples teach you?

To exalt God — John 9:3

What reason did Jesus give for the man's blindness? See John 9:3.

How was this reason fulfilled by what Jesus did? See John 9:6 – 7, 13 – 33.

How does Peter expand this answer in 1 Peter 1:6 – 7?

How was this reason experienced by Jesus Himself? See Hebrews 5:8 – 9; John 17:1 – 5.

What physical, social, emotional, intellectual, or mental limitations do you have? How could they be opportunities for God to display Himself to others through your life?

What other opportunities to exalt God do you see in your life? How will you act on them today?

To embrace daylight — John 9:4 – 5

Write John 9:4 in your own words.

What similar thought do you find in John 4:27 – 35; 2 Timothy 4:1 – 6; Romans 13:11 – 14?

What is the "daylight" in your life?

What is God asking you to do now that you may not be able to do in five years? In ten years? In twenty years?

How can you take advantage of the "daylight" in the way you spend your time? Your money? Your energy?

SEIZE THE OPPORTUNITY

To do something — John 9:6

What did Jesus do about what He saw? See John 9:6 – 7.

How are we to respond to the needs of others? See James 2:14 – 18; Luke 10:30 – 37; Mark 9:36 – 37, 41; Proverbs 3:27 – 28.

List the things you are doing to help those in need.

What is God calling you to do today for someone in need?

To change someone — John 9:7

What difference did Jesus make in the blind man's life? See John 9:8 – 38.

What difference should our actions make, according to Matthew 5:14 – 16? Compare John 13:35 to 1 John 3:16 – 18.

Name at least one person who trusts or loves Jesus more because of something you have done or said.

What opportunity do you need to seize "while it is day" (John 9:4 KJV) in order to make an eternal difference in someone's life?

Don't miss something very important God wants to do in your life, or through you in someone else's life, because you aren't on His schedule. Five minutes before "nightfall," what will you wish you had done? Get on His schedule and do it!

What Time Is It?

A re we mindful of the biblical guideposts that signal the end of the age?

On December 26, 2004, the earth's plates separated, then collided somewhere deep beneath the Indian Ocean, producing an earthquake of 9.0 on the Richter scale. Within hours a giant wall of water crashed onto the shores of a dozen countries, leaving death and devastation in its wake. Commentators called it a disaster of biblical proportions. The worldwide relief effort was the largest in human history.

"Is this a sign of the end of the world?" is a question I have heard repeatedly after a natural disaster, from believers and unbelievers alike. It's an important question to ponder because Jesus told the people of His day, "You know how to interpret the appearance of the sky, but you cannot interpret the signs of the times."[13] Jesus wanted His disciples — and you and me — to know how to "tell time."

---

13. Matthew 16:3.

THE TIME IS LATE

In Matthew 24:1 – 2, as Jesus looked over Jerusalem, He lamented that the city would be destroyed completely, a prophecy that was fulfilled in AD 70. The disciples then asked Him two questions: "When will this happen," and "What will be the sign of your coming and of the end of the age?" (Matthew 24:3). It was the second question that Jesus answered by giving signs which would indicate the end of human history as we have known it. I have divided the signs into four categories.

Signs in the spiritual (religious) world

What warning did Jesus give in Matthew 24:4? How many times does Jesus refer to this danger in Matthew 24? Give phrases and verse numbers for each.

Give the phrase that repeats this warning in 2 Thessalonians 2:3.

Give some examples of how people today — especially religious people — are being deceived in regard to the end of the world and the coming of Christ.

From Matthew 24:5 – 12, give at least five signs of the end of the age (in the religious realm) and a contemporary example of each.

Signs from the nations of the world

What are two signs Jesus gave regarding the world's nations in Matthew 24:6 – 7a?

What is another sign regarding the nations in Luke 21:25?

Give examples of these signs being fulfilled today.

Signs in the natural world

Give signs from the world of nature in Matthew 24:7b; Luke 21:11, 25.

List examples of these signs that have occurred in our world during the past year.

Signs in the social world

What happened in Noah's day? See Genesis 6:5 – 14; 7:11 – 12, 17 – 23 for your answer.

Is there anything wrong with "eating and drinking, marrying and giving in marriage" (Matthew 24:38)? What was the real problem with Noah's generation?

How does Peter use this same analogy in 2 Peter 3:5 – 6?

What similarities do you see between Noah's generation and ours?

What are some other signs in the social world from James 5:3? From 2 Timothy 3:1 – 5? Give examples of each.

THE TIME IS SHORT

In Matthew 24:8, Jesus used "birth pains" to describe these signs. Birth pains occur at intervals of increasing frequency and with increasing intensity. While the signs Jesus gave always have been present in our world, when we see them increasing in frequency and intensity, the Scripture says, "Lift up your heads, because your redemption is drawing near" (Luke 21:28).

- From Matthew 24:14, what is perhaps the most exciting sign of all?

- How is this sign uniquely being fulfilled in our generation?

- What are you doing to help bring this to pass?

THE TIME IS NOW

To watch

What do you think Jesus means by "keep watch" in Matthew 24:42?

Why is this important, according to Matthew 24:42 – 44?

What are some practical things you can do to "keep watch"?

To work

From Matthew 24:45 – 47, what does Jesus want to find you and me doing when He returns?

If He returns in the next five minutes, what will He find you doing?

Take a moment now to ask Him to give you a work assignment — something you can do that will make an eternal difference in the kingdom of God.

To walk

What does Jesus not want to find us doing, according to Matthew 24:48 – 51?

What are several things we are to do, in light of the imminent return of Christ, from 1 Peter 4:7; 2 Peter 3:11 – 12, 14, 17 – 18; 1 Thessalonians 4:11 – 12?

How should the hope of the return of Christ make an impact on our lives, according to 1 John 3:3? Can you give an example of this from your own life?

From Ephesians 4:1 – 3, describe a walk that is pleasing to God. How does your walk compare?

What are some practical things you can do to adjust your walk to keep pace with His?

With my busy schedule, knowing the accurate time is critical. Catching a plane, speaking in a pulpit, talking in front of a television camera — even cooking dinner — all of these activities require an awareness of time. Almost every room in my house has a clock, several of which are radio-controlled, so that the time is accurate to the second. And I would never travel without my radio-controlled alarm. Without them, I may be "deceived" into missing an appointment — or burning the pot roast.

Don't be deceived as to what time it is in human history. Know the signs, read your newspaper, and be ready. Learn how to tell time. Jesus is coming! Soon!

November

GRATITUDE

Thanksliving

Thanksgiving is my favorite holiday of the year. I look forward to the whole family — all who can join us — celebrating Thanksgiving together. I enjoy the abundant, delicious feast — turkey with dressing and gravy, ham, green beans, corn pudding, sweet potato casseroles, pies with real whipped cream, sweet iced tea. My mouth waters just thinking about it!

But the highlight of our Thanksgiving is the fellowship around the dining room table as each one shares what he or she is most thankful for. As precious as those moments are, I am convicted that our gratitude to God is not meant to be measured out once a year around a dining room table. It is to be translated into genuine "thanksliving."

The concept of thanksliving seemed to escape the early Israelites. They had been delivered from bondage in Egypt by the supernatural power of God. Yet within days of their deliverance, they apparently had forgotten His power and, in terror, were blaming Him for delivering them from Egypt so they could die in the desert.[14] Instead of letting them die, once again God exerted His mighty power, parting the Red Sea so that the Israelites crossed safely on dry ground while the pursuing Egyptian army was annihilated.

Shortly thereafter, when they became hungry, instead of asking God to provide for their needs, they whined in self-pity that it would have been better to die in Egypt as well-fed slaves! God, nonetheless, met their needs by sending fresh manna every morning.

---

14. See Exodus 14:11.

For the next forty years, as the Israelites wandered in the wilderness, they whined and complained. Their focus always seemed to be on themselves and on their immediate problems, instead of on the God who had delivered, cared for, and guided them.

Finally, all but two of the men who had walked out of Egypt were dead. God called Joshua to lead the second generation of freed Israelite slaves out of the wilderness and into the Promised Land. Once again, the Israelites experienced God's power as He rolled back the waters of the Jordan River, enabling them to cross over on dry ground and take possession of all that God had for them. And to help ensure that the Israelites did not regress into the old pattern of whining doubt and complaining unbelief, they were challenged in a unique way to keep their focus on God through thanksliving.

Read Joshua 3 and 4

LITERAL THANKS

Where did the stones of remembrance come from? See Joshua 4:2 – 3, 5, 8.

In Joshua 4:6 – 7, why did God say that the stones were to be collected and carried to the riverbank?

What has God done for you as recently as this past week for which you have yet to thank Him?

What are some practical, literal things you can do to help remember what God has done for you, in order to cultivate and maintain an attitude of gratitude?

From the following passages, describe other visuals God gave His people and what each represented: Genesis 9:12 – 16; Exodus 12:1 – 13; Matthew 26:26 – 29; John 20:24 – 29.

LIVING THANKS

What was necessary before the Israelites could experience God's power? See Joshua 4:10.

What was the living proof of God's power?

What do you think the crossing of the Jordan symbolizes in the Christian life?

Did the Israelites believe that their experience of God's power meant their lives would be easy from then on? Give a verse to prove your point.

What is significant in Joshua 4:18? How would this affect the Israelites?

Who are the "living stones today," and what is one of their primary purposes? Compare 1 Peter 2:4 – 5 with 1 Peter 2:9. Also compare Ephesians 2:19 – 22 with Ephesians 1:4 – 6.

LASTING THANKS

What did the stones mean? See Joshua 4:22 – 24.

What were the Israelites to do with the memories of their experiences of God's power? Read Joshua 4:6 – 7, 22.

When others look at your life, do they demand an explanation for what they see? What explanation do you give them?

What object could you place in your home or office that would be a conversation starter, giving you the opportunity to tell others about your experiences of God's power?

What testimony are you leaving behind for your children or grandchildren? How will you be sure they get it?

What are at least two reasons for us to give verbal testimony to what God has done for us? See Joshua 4:24; Luke 1:1 – 4; John 4:28 – 42; 20:30 – 31; 1 John 1:1 – 4.

How do nine of the ten lepers in Luke 17:11 – 19 illustrate living thanks but not lasting thanks? How does the one leper illustrate both living and lasting thanks?

During His triumphant entry into Jerusalem on Palm Sunday, Jesus proclaimed that if those who love Him did not praise Him, the stones would cry out! Why would you and I allow a stone to have the privilege that is ours? Has a self-centered focus silenced your praise this Thanksgiving? Complete the following sentence with as many attributes of God as you can: I praise God for His _____.

Celebrate Thanksgiving this month, but practice thanksliving every day throughout the year.

Jesus Is Enough

This month we will celebrate Thanksgiving once again. It's one of my very favorite days of the year because the focus is truly on all that I have to be thankful for.

What will you be thanking God for this month?

- Your physical health ... or His faithfulness to see you through sickness?
- Your financial health ... or His wisdom to help you navigate and avoid financial disaster?
- Your family and friends who have stayed with you through good times and bad ... or His comfort to ease the pain when you've been abandoned?
- Your church that has helped you stay focused on Him because they encouraged you by their love ... or His support as you regained your focus in spite of failure or betrayal?

As I think through the things for which I am truly thankful, I sometimes wonder if my list of "thanks" is superseded by my list of "wants." Just walking through the mall can deceive me into thinking that I don't have "enough." In the world of consumerism in which we live, am I discontented with what I have? Are you? How many of us are actually so satisfied that we think we have "enough"?

Read Genesis 1 and Colossians 1:15 – 23

As children of God, we have been blessed with every spiritual blessing in Christ. But if we were absolutely honest in our confession, would we truly say that "Jesus is enough"?

Who is God, according to: Genesis 1:1, 27; Isaiah 40:28; 44:24; John 4:24; 1 Timothy 4:10?

Give characteristics that reveal He is a living person. See Genesis 2:7, 16, 21 – 22; 3:8; 4:16; 6:6; 11:5. (Example: He breathes. Genesis 2:7.)

How many gods are there in the universe? See 1 Corinthians 8:6. What is the significance of that?

Has anyone ever seen God? See 1 John 4:12. What is the significance of that?

Through whom has He revealed Himself? See Hebrews 1:1 – 3; John 1:18; 14:8 – 9; Colossians 1:15. How is that like seeing God?

In 1 John 4:12; John 1:18; and Colossians 2:9, when Bible characters claimed to have "seen" God, whom were they actually seeing?

Can a person worship God without honoring Jesus Christ as His unique Son (such as God-fearing Muslims or Jews)? Give key phrases from John 5:19 – 23.

ENOUGH IN HIS AUTHORITY

Who is the Creator? Name one thing He did not create. See Colossians 1:16 – 17; Ephesians 3:9; Revelation 4:11.

What two "agents" of power does God use in creation that He still uses today? Compare Genesis 1:2 with Acts 1:8; and Genesis 1:3 with Hebrews 4:12 and Revelation 1:16.

How many times does the phrase "and God said," or the equivalent, occur in Genesis 1? Give the verses.

Was "and God said" more than just a phrase of language? What explanation does John 1:1 – 3, 14 give?

What preparation has to take place before the power of God's Word can bring about change? See Genesis 1:2; Acts 1:8; John 3:5 – 8.

ENOUGH IN HIS SUPREMACY

Who is the most important person in the universe? Give phrases from Colossians 1:15 – 19.

Is there anyone in the universe with greater authority? Give phrases from Matthew 28:18; Ephesians 1:19 – 23; John 17:2.

What is His position, according to Ephesians 1:20; Revelation 5:6, 13; and Isaiah 6:1 with John 12:41?

ENOUGH IN HIS ACTIVITY

What is God's purpose for you? See Colossians 1:20 – 23; Ephesians 1:4 – 8; Romans 8:29. Compare Genesis 1:28 with Ephesians 1:3.

How is His purpose accomplished in your life? Give the steps:

1. Romans 3:23; 1 John 1:9

2. Luke 13:3, 5; Acts 2:38; 3:19

3. John 3:16; Romans 10:9 – 10; 3:22

4. Revelation 3:20; John 1:12

5. Ephesians 1:13 – 14; 1 Corinthians 6:11

6. Romans 12:1 – 2; 2 Corinthians 3:18; 1 John 3:1 – 3

7. Philippians 1:6

How is it possible to know God personally? Compare John 3:16 with John 10:10, 27–30 and John 17:3. Do you know God personally?

If Jesus is God in human flesh, revealing to us exactly what God is like . . .

If Jesus holds the highest position in the universe, and everything and everyone is subject to His authority . . .

If Jesus is greater than anyone or anything in the visible or invisible world . . .

If Jesus has a purpose that He is actively completing in the universe as well as in your own life . . .

Then *He is enough*!

This Thanksgiving, make the time to thank God for Jesus.

He *is* enough!

Hurricane Katrina would have been fearsome as a stand-alone hurricane, but the breaking of the levees in New Orleans and the unprecedented flooding and human misery that followed have given her notoriety as the worst natural disaster in our nation's history and the worst overall disaster since the Civil War.

When disaster strikes, how are God's people supposed to respond besides weeping? Giving to the relief effort? Opening our homes? Volunteering our time? Are all commendable options.

But there is one thing God's people can do more effectively than anyone else. Pray. The Old Testament prophet Habakkuk set a clear example for us. He knew the mounting sin in his nation was pushing God beyond the limits of His patience. When God confirmed that His judgment would fall in the form of a disaster so catastrophic that Habakkuk wouldn't believe it if he heard it,[15] Habakkuk turned to God and poured out his heart in prayer.

As we listen to Habakkuk pray, we learn that when disaster strikes, we need to turn to God and keep our focus on Him.

---

15. See Habakkuk 1:5.

Read Habakkuk 3

STAY FOCUSED ON GOD'S AVAILABILITY — Hab. 3:1

What disaster has struck you or a loved one?

Write the phrases of encouragement that you find in the following verses: Isaiah 43:1 – 4; Psalm 46:1 – 7; 91:14 – 16; 145:18; 1 Peter 3:12.

Describe other situations when people have turned to God during a disaster. See Genesis 18:16 – 23; 2 Chronicles 20:1 – 6, 12; Nehemiah 1:1 – 4.

STAY FOCUSED ON GOD'S CONSISTENCY — Hab. 3:2

From each of the following passages, describe God's awesome deeds: Genesis 1:1 – 31; 6:11 – 8:22; Exodus 14:5 – 31; Joshua 6:1 – 20; 1 Samuel 17:1 – 50; 1 Kings 18:16 – 39; Daniel 3:1 – 30; 6:1 – 28.

Put Habakkuk's request of God into your own words. See Habakkuk 3:2.

Do you think God's power has been diluted over the years? See Isaiah 59:1; Hebrews 13:8.

What has God done for you in the past that you want Him to do again?

Describe God's glory from the following verses: Psalm 19:1–6; Job 38:1–12, 16, 19, 22–24, 28–30, 32, 36; Exodus 15:11–13; 24:15–17; 34:29–35; 40:34–35; Habakkuk 3:3–4; John 1:1–3, 14.

How was God's glory revealed through disaster in John 17:1–5; 1 Peter 1:6–9?

STAY FOCUSED ON GOD'S MAJESTY — Hab. 3:5–6

How does Isaiah describe God's majesty in Isaiah 40:21–31?

Give other aspects of God's majesty from Exodus 15:6, 11; Isaiah 26:10; Habakkuk 3:5–6; 2 Thessalonians 1:8–10; Psalm 29:4; 111:3; Ephesians 1:19–23; Matthew 28:18–20.

Give one demonstration of His power in your life.

STAY FOCUSED ON GOD'S ETERNITY — Hab. 3:6b

Write your own definition of eternity. See John 17:3; Revelation 1:8.

Give phrases from the following verses that describe God's eternity: Deuteronomy 33:27; Psalm 16:11; 21:6; 111:10; 119:89, 160; Isaiah 26:4; Jeremiah 10:10; Daniel 4:3, 34; Romans 1:20.

When disaster strikes, what does it mean to you that God and His ways are eternal? See John 3:16; 4:14; 5:24; 6:40; 10:28.

STAY FOCUSED ON GOD'S AUTHORITY — Hab. 3:7 – 16

From Habakkuk 3:7 – 16, list the personal pronouns "you" and "your," along with the nouns, adjectives, adverbs, and verbs that immediately follow.

What encouragement does this give you?

Read Luke 5:21 – 26; John 5:26 – 27; Romans 12:19; Revelation 18:20; 19:1 – 2, 11 – 16; 17:13 – 14; 12:10. What further encouragement do you receive from these verses, especially in times of disaster?

STAY FOCUSED ON GOD'S SUFFICIENCY — Hab. 3:17 – 19

Write an application for each of the difficult situations in Habakkuk 3:17.

What's the worst thing that could happen to you or to the person you're praying for?

According to Habakkuk 3:18, what was Habakkuk's choice at the conclusion of his prayer? Give phrases.

How are we instructed to make that same choice in Psalm 43:1 – 5; Philippians 4:4, 11 – 12; Hebrews 13:5?

As his national situation worsened, on what did Habakkuk rely, according to Habakkuk 3:19?

What phrase indicates Habakkuk was determined to live by faith, not somehow, but triumphantly?

When disaster strikes nationally, locally, or personally, what encouragement do you receive from 2 Chronicles 7:13 – 15; 2 Peter 1:3 – 4; 2 Corinthians 12:7 – 10?

If God doesn't _____, yet I will praise Him. Fill in the blank.

This month, as you celebrate Thanksgiving, stay focused on God. Express your gratitude for His blessings by spending sincere, heartfelt time in prayer — especially for those experiencing disaster.

I Saw the Lord

I have been asked very skeptically, "Anne, you mean you've seen the Lord? Where?" And I've answered with a deep, confident knowing, "Yes, I've seen the Lord … during the hard times in my life. Dryness and darkness. Trial and turmoil. Storm and suffering. 'Clouds' that obscure everything and everyone else … except the Lord."

What bad thing has swept into your life, rendering you helpless? Death? Divorce? Disease? Debt? Instead of being delivered, did your loved one die from cancer?

Has …

- a feud erupted in your family?
- a betrayal occurred in your marriage?
- a rebellion challenged your parenting?
- an untimely end come to your pregnancy?
- a severance taken you from your job?
- a military deployment deprived you of loved ones?

Besides feeling totally helpless, what was your reaction? Are you defiantly standing in the midst of the swirling circumstances, yelling in your spirit, "Why did You let this bad thing happen?" Or maybe you're withdrawing into a shell of denial and depression, hoping things won't get any worse.

I heard that a turkey and an eagle react differently to the threat of a storm. A turkey runs under the barn, hoping the storm won't come near. An eagle leaves the security of its nest, spreads its wings, and rides the air currents of the storm, knowing its wings and the air currents will carry it higher in the sky than it could soar on its own. Based on your reaction to what has happened in your life, which are you — a turkey or an eagle?

It's natural for me to be a turkey in my emotions, but I have chosen to be an eagle in my spirit. And as I have spread my wings of faith to embrace the "wind," placing my trust in Jesus and Jesus alone, I have experienced quiet "everyday" miracles:

His joy has balanced my pain.

His power has lifted my burden.

His peace has calmed my worries.

His grace has been more than adequate to cover me.

His strength has been sufficient to carry me through.

His love has bathed my wounds like a healing balm ...

And through it all, I have seen the Lord!

Read Exodus 33 and 34

SEE THE LORD IN THE DESERT

Describe a spiritual desert. See Exodus 15:22; 16:2 – 3.

Where did God's people see the Lord in Exodus 16:10?

Describe John's "desert" in Revelation 1:9. What was his experience there, according to Revelation 1:9 – 16?

Can you think of a time when you were spiritually dry, cut off from all that was familiar, yet you met God in a fresh way?

How are you encouraged by Isaiah 35:6; Exodus 17:1 – 6; Genesis 21:14 – 20?

SEE THE LORD IN THE DARKNESS

When have you floundered in the darkness of confusion or temptation, disappointment or depression?

What did God promise His people in Exodus 19:9?

How was Jonah in the dark, and what was his testimony in Jonah 2:1 – 3:2? The psalmist in Psalm 40:2? Daniel in Daniel 6:1 – 28? Lazarus in John 11:14, 33 – 35, 38 – 44?

How are you encouraged by Exodus 20:21; Psalm 97:2; 2 Samuel 22:29?

SEE THE LORD IN THE STORM

What storms of disease, death, divorce, disaster, or other upheavals have come into your life? See Proverbs 1:27.

Describe Ezekiel's storm in Ezekiel 1:1 – 5. Whom did he see in Ezekiel 1:25 – 28?

Describe the storm and the unique experience of the three young Hebrew men in Daniel 3:1 – 25.

Describe Peter's storm in Matthew 14:22 – 33. What did he discover as a result?

What do you learn about storms from these descriptions? From Job 40:6; Proverbs 10:25; Nahum 1:3?

What does Jesus teach you from His own example in Luke 8:22 – 25?

SEE THE LORD ON THE MOUNTAIN

While I understand that mountains can represent peaks and high points in our lives, they can also represent difficulties, obstacles, hardship, and stress because of the effort required to climb them.

Name some mountains in your life right now.

How are you encouraged by Exodus 34:1 – 5? By Genesis 22:14; Mark 9:2 – 8?

The Bible says, "Now we see through a glass, darkly; but then face to face."[16]

Ask God to give you eyes to see the Lord even now in the midst of your desert, darkness, storm, and mountain-sized hardship. Then open your eyes and look.

---

16. 1 Corinthians 13:12 KJV.

December

CHRIST

The Real Meaning of Christmas

Our culture is becoming increasingly secularized — there seems to be a broad range of people who do not know who Jesus truly is. Yet this December, most of the world will celebrate His birth. Who is Jesus …

… that some of the greatest architectural achievements in Europe were built in which to worship Him?

… that some of the world's most beautiful art and music were created to honor and praise Him?

… that less than four hundred years after Rome crucified Him, He was acknowledged as the only god in the Roman Empire?

… that Alexander Solzhenitsyn, rotting in a Siberian work camp, says the very thought of Him was enough to keep his sanity?

… that people all over the world say He has saved them from drugs, illness, suicide, depression, or other ills?

… that in His name, people forsake personal gain to feed the hungry, house the homeless, clothe the naked, and heal the sick?

Why is Jesus so offensive to some and so pleasing to others? So wrong to some and so right to others? So controversial to some and so necessary to others?

In the midst of all the busyness, loneliness, religiousness, and happiness, would you celebrate the real meaning of Christmas this year by keeping your focus on who Jesus is?

HE IS THE INCARNATION OF GOD'S GREATNESS — John 1:1 – 4

Who is the Word that John 1:1 refers to? See John 1:14.

He is the same as God

What is the significance of the presence of the Word in John 1:1? How does Colossians 1:17 affirm this? Relate this to His birth in Bethlehem. See Matthew 1:18, 22 – 23.

Give at least four characteristics of the Word in John 1:1 – 3. Put into your own words what each characteristic means.

Because Jesus Christ is God's living Word, what added insight does Matthew 12:34b give? What does this mean to you?

He is the source of life

Where does the world say life comes from? What impact does this have on a person's view of human life?

Where does God's Word say life comes from? Give specific phrases from Genesis 1:1 – 27; 2:7 and Colossians 1:16. How does knowledge of this truth change a person's value of human life?

He is the significance of life

Read John 1:4. How does His life give your life light or significance?

When you are born physically, what is your spiritual state, according to Ephesians 2:1? Are there any exceptions? See Romans 3:23. What does this mean? Relate this to Romans 6:23; John 5:24.

Describe in your own words when you passed from death into life.

HE IS THE INCARNATION OF GOD'S GOSPEL — John 1:5–13

From each of the following verses, give one aspect of the gospel: Romans 3:23; 6:23; John 1:12; 3:16; 14:6; Acts 4:12; 1 John 1:9; Romans 10:9–10; Revelation 3:20; Ephesians 1:13–14; Hebrews 13:5.

Rejected by many

What were two responses to Christ's coming, according to John 1:10–11?

Give examples of people who respond to Christ in the same way today.

Received by some

Biblical names were more than just a word — they often revealed character. Give examples of meaningful names from the following verses: Genesis 17:5; 32:28; Matthew 16:17–18.

Give the meaning of each of the following names: "Lord" from John 20:28; "Jesus" from Matthew 1:21; "Christ" from Matthew 26:63.

What do you think it means in John 1:12 to believe in His "name"?

What do you think is the difference between "believing" and "receiving"? Are both required in order for a person to become a child of God?

Based on the prerequisites in John 1:12 – 13, does God recognize you as His child?

HE IS THE INCARNATION OF GOD'S GLORY — John 1:14 – 15

Describe Moses' glimpse of God's glory from Exodus 33:18 – 23.

How did Moses' glimpse of God's glory differ from the shepherds' experience in Luke 2:8 – 20? The wise men's experience in Matthew 2:1 – 12? John's experience in John 1:14?

HE IS THE INCARNATION OF GOD'S GRACE — John 1:16 – 18

Grace refers to the blessings of God that we don't deserve. It has been defined by this acrostic: Great Riches At Christ's Expense.

Name some of God's blessings you don't deserve that give evidence of the fullness of His grace as referred to in John 1:16. See also Ephesians 1:3.

What was the basic purpose of God's law? Compare John 1:17 with Galatians 3:19 – 25.

What was the effect of the law? See Ephesians 2:1 – 3.

How does grace deliver us from the law's condemnation? See Ephesians 2:4 – 9.

Write John 1:18 in simple words that a child can understand.

When you "look" at Jesus, what or who do you "see"?

Would you celebrate Christmas by maintaining, throughout the holidays, your genuine worship of Christ? Who is He? He is God wrapped in swaddling clothes, lying in a manger. He is the Creator who became your Savior.

Catching the Christmas Spirit

How do you and I catch the Christmas spirit if we're not in the mood for Christmas? Should we decorate the house? Plan Christmas parties? Take gifts to the underprivileged?

What happens when you just can't psych yourself up for Christmas? The answer is simple. We get excited about Christmas by sharing Christ.

Read Luke 2:8 – 20

KNOW THE MEANING OF CHRISTMAS

What does Christmas mean to you? See Luke 2:1 – 20.

Heaven is opened

Describe the circumstances in Genesis 3:1 – 24 that originally closed the door to God's presence, shutting out the people on earth.

Describe the people who first heard that Christ had come to "open" heaven, in Luke 2:8 – 9.

Where were they and what were they doing? What does this mean to you?

To whom has heaven been opened, according to the angel in Luke 2:10? See also Revelation 21:25 – 27; 22:17.

Relate this to Genesis 28:10 – 12; John 1:47 – 51; 14:6. Who is the "ladder" that spans the gulf between heaven and earth, between God and man?

Heaven is offered

When heaven was opened, who was revealed? See Luke 2:11.

What does the name "Jesus" mean? See Matthew 1:21.

Look up the definitions for "Lord" and "Christ" and write the definitions as they apply to Jesus.

What was the good news of Christ's coming, as related to heaven being closed since the beginning of human history?

What was the purpose of this first Christmas morning? See Luke 2:13 – 14.

Write in your own words what Christmas means, according to Luke 2.

What is the miracle of Christmas?

Compelled by an awareness of emptiness

Describe the dramatic visual, physical, and emotional contrast between Luke 2:3 – 14 and Luke 2:15.

How do you think the shepherds felt initially when the angels left?

Have you ever had a feeling of letdown or extreme loneliness around Christmas? How have you responded to that feeling? Are you trying to maintain the emotion of Christmas or are you focused on the message?

Compelled by an attitude of expectancy

How did the shepherds respond to the good news? See Luke 2:16.

Why did the shepherds drop everything and hurry off to find the baby?

How was the promise of Luke 2:12 fulfilled in Luke 2:16? How does this also confirm Jeremiah 29:13; Proverbs 8:17?

Use your imagination to write a description of Luke 2:16, including the search, the scene, and the stunning privilege of staring into the face of God.

What time and effort will you make to "find the baby" in the midst of your Christmas celebration?

What will you do to help someone find Him this Christmas?

GO AND TELL THE MESSAGE OF CHRISTMAS

What is the message of Christmas? See John 3:16 – 17.

Personally

What phrase tells you this encounter with Jesus was a personal one? See Luke 2:17.

Following their encounter with the baby, what did the shepherds do? See Luke 2:17 – 18.

How does the shepherds' personal encounter with the baby relate to 1 John 1:1 – 3; John 1:1 – 2, 14; Acts 4:20?

What difference does it make if your witness is based on secondhand hearsay or a personal, firsthand experience?

Patiently

Of all those who were "amazed" at the shepherds' testimony in Luke 2:18, how many does the Scripture say went to see the baby for themselves?

Do you think the lack of response indicates there was something wrong with the shepherds' witness? Why or why no
How many people do you know who celebrate Christmas without "seeing" the baby for themselves? Do you think this is good or bad? Why?

How is this lack of "seeing" addressed in Acts 28:23 – 31; 2 Timothy 4:2 – 5; Hebrews 6:12; 10:36?

If you have shared the Christ of Christmas but have had no positive response, how are you encouraged by Acts 28:23 – 31; 2 Timothy 4:16 – 18; Hebrews 12:1 – 3; Galatians 6:9?

With praise

How were the shepherds' practical circumstances the same after they had seen the baby? How were they different?

What evidence is there in Luke 2:20 that the shepherds had caught the Christmas spirit?

Will Luke 2:20 be a description of your attitude on December 26? If not, why?

What phrase in Luke 2:20 describes the total confidence the shepherds had in what they had seen and heard, regardless of the response of others?

Is there any part of the Christmas story that you doubt? What is it, and why? What will you do now to resolve that doubt so that you can tell others the good news of Christmas with confident joy?

Once you know the true meaning of Christmas, then catch the Christmas spirit by going into stores, schools, businesses, offices, neighborhoods, and churches, telling everyone that "A Savior has been born to you; He is Christ the Lord" ... a Savior who has opened heaven, offering it to everyone who will believe and receive Him.

His Star

When you leaf through a magazine, what makes you stop at certain pages? What gets your attention? Is it the title? The graphic? When you go to the mall, what causes you to stop and browse in a particular department? Is it the display of items? The colors? The fragrance? What makes you pause your channel surfing to watch a particular television commercial? Is it the sound of the music or the announcer's voice?

Our senses are bombarded 24/7 by thousands of sounds and sights. Marketing companies spend significant amounts of money to determine how to get our attention for whatever they are trying to sell or promote. Politicians have highly paid staff members who do nothing but analyze how to get publicity for their candidates so that we will be drawn to vote for them.

I wonder ... what would I have used to get the world to turn aside and look at a tiny baby? How could I turn the world's attention to an infant wrapped in swaddling clothes and lying in a manger in a stable behind some inn in an obscure Judean town? A trumpet blast? A lightning bolt? A thunderous announcement from Mount Sinai?

When God wanted to get the attention of His own people to look into His own infant face, He sent angels. When He wanted to get the attention of the nations of the world, wrapped up in their own religious traditions and belief systems, He used a star.

Read Matthew 2:1 – 12

Not in a religion

Who was seeking Jesus in Matthew 2:1?

Some scholars describe the Magi as astronomers. If so, what does this tell you about who they were?

Using a map, name the nations east of Jerusalem.

Describe some of the religious practices of the eastern nations. See Daniel 3:1 – 8; Jeremiah 51:47.

What do these practices tell you about the religious background of the Magi?

What implies that the Magi were restless in their religious experience and yearning for something more?

Who do you know who is looking for something more than their own experience or religious tradition?

In a relationship

What did God use to get the attention of the Magi? See Matthew 2:2.

How does God use similar means to get the attention of those outside the church today? Give phrases from Psalm 19:1 – 4; Romans 1:20.

What are some other "stars" God uses to get the world's attention? Consider Matthew 5:16 and 7:15 – 20 along with John 15:8; Mark 16:15; Acts 8:6.

How do you think the Magi knew the King of the Jews had arrived? Given Daniel's position in Babylon, what prophetic writings might the Magi have studied? See Daniel 5:10 – 12.

When have you invited unsaved persons to your church or Bible study where they can hear God's Word for themselves?

What was the stated purpose of the Magi in seeking Jesus?

This Christmas, ask God to make you a "star" that leads others to seek Him through your words and life.

In spite of political hostility

How did the political leadership react to the stated purpose of the Magi? See Matthew 2:3.

What proof is there that Herod was lying in Matthew 2:7 – 8? See Matthew 2:13 – 18.

Do you know people who pretend to be interested in Jesus for their own hidden agenda?

Why do you think political leaders, governments, and even entire cultures are threatened by Jesus and those who seek to worship Him? See Matthew 28:18; Ephesians 1:22.

Name some efforts to eliminate Jesus from our society. Do you think it's possible for them to be successful? Why?

In spite of public animosity

What was the public's reaction in Matthew 2:3?

Why do you think the public was disturbed?

In Matthew 2:3, who seemed to set the agenda for what was or was not politically correct?

How does this relate to our world today?

Read John 15:18 – 27; Matthew 10:18 – 20; 1 Peter 2:23; 4:19; Acts 4:18 – 21; Matthew 5:11 – 12. As you seek to lead others to Jesus and face political hostility and public animosity, how do these verses encourage you?

In spite of religious hypocrisy

Did the religious leaders know the Scriptures? See Matthew 2:4 – 6.

Although they were religious, what evidence is there that they did not actually believe, apply, or obey the Scriptures?

What blessings did they miss because of their unbelief?

What do Matthew 7:21 – 23; Isaiah 29:13; Malachi 2:7 – 9; and Revelation 3:14 – 20 say about religious hypocrisy?

What was one positive thing that the religious leaders' knowledge of Scripture enabled them to do?

In spite of personal conformity

Read Matthew 2:9. What did the Magi do that no one else in Jerusalem did?

How did God encourage them in Matthew 2:10?

What encouragement have you given to someone who has stepped away from the crowd to seek a personal relationship with Jesus?

Explain the encouragement you receive from the actions of the men in the following examples: Genesis 6:5 – 9; 12:1 – 4; Hebrews 11:24 – 27; Daniel 1:1 – 20; 3:1 – 30; 6:1 – 28. When they refused to conform, what blessing was in store for each of them? What blessing was in store for the Magi?

HIS STAR LEADS PEOPLE TO WORSHIP HIM

On what did the star focus in Matthew 2:9? When witnessing to those outside the church, what is your focus?

How was Peter's focus similar in Acts 2:22 – 24 and 3:1 – 6?

How was Paul's focus similar in 1 Corinthians 1:17 and 2:2?

In Matthew 2:11, where did the Magi's long journey lead?

When the Magi saw Jesus, how did they react? Describe in your own words the scene in Matthew 2:11.

The Magi gave Jesus three gifts: gold; incense, which was used in ceremonial prayer; and myrrh, an embalming spice. How does each gift represent who Jesus is? Give phrases from the following verses that correspond with each gift: Revelation 19:16; Hebrews 8:1 – 2; and Matthew 1:21 with Luke 9:22.

Do you think the Magi would have sought, found, and worshiped Jesus without His star? Why or why not?

Whom do you know who will never seek, find, or worship Jesus without a "star" to guide them?

This Christmas, as you hang stars on your Christmas tree, make star-shaped cookies, and immerse yourself in holiday activities, ask God to use you to draw the attention of others to the baby in the manger. "Those who are wise will shine like the brightness of the heavens, and those who lead many to righteousness, like the stars for ever and ever."[17] This Christmas, be His star!

17. Daniel 12:3.

A Gift for the King

Every year I wrestle with what to give my father for Christmas. He seems to have everything he wants or needs. And so I mentally search for ideas, weeks in advance. Around Thanksgiving I usually give up and just ask him what he would like.

In similar fashion, I approach the Christmas holidays wondering what I should give the King of Kings. What do you give Someone who truly does have everything? So I always ask the King what He would like from me.

He has been very creative in His requests! They vary widely, but they have two things in common: The gift is always sacrificial in nature, something I would not do unless the King requested it. And it is something I could not do except that the King enabled me.

One year He seemed to ask for my involvement in carrying out the last request of an executed murderer. One year He requested that I add a trip of multiple speaking engagements to my already completed schedule. Another year He prompted me to tell the Christmas story in my child's public school classroom.

What will you give the King this Christmas? Ask Him what He would like to receive from you. The following is a gift that I know He would like to receive.

Read John 13:1 – 17

SERVICE OFFERED LOVINGLY — John 13:1 – 11

What phrase from John 13:1 indicates Jesus knew that He would be arrested and crucified within a few hours of this dinner scene?

Knowing what was facing Him shortly, what could have been Jesus' mental and emotional state?

Describe in your own words the "full extent of his love" referred to in this passage. Relate this to John 15:13 as well as to the dinner scene that follows in John 13:1 – 11.

To what extent do you love Jesus? Are there any limitations to your love that are acceptable to Him? See Romans 12:1 – 2.

What excuse do you have for offering service with an unloving attitude? What can you do to serve more consistently in love?

What boundaries have you placed on your love for others?

From the following verses, summarize how or why it is important — in His eyes — for you to love others: Matthew 22:37 – 39; Mark 12:33; Luke 6:32 – 35; John 13:34 – 35; 15:12, 16 – 17; 17:11, 26; Galatians 5:13; 1 John 4:7 – 12.

SERVICE OFFERED WILLINGLY — John 13:2 – 3

What phrase indicates that Jesus had a right to expect to be served? See John 13:2 – 3.

Was this a convenient time for Him to serve? Explain.

Did everyone at the table appreciate His service? Give a verse or phrase to support your answer.

What simple act of service have you refrained from because you expect to be served?

What service have you refused to offer because it's not a convenient time, it's not your job, and no one appreciates it anyway? Compare your refusal to His willingness.

SERVICE OFFERED HUMBLY — John 13:4 – 11

From Luke 22:24 – 27, what was the subject of conversation among the disciples just prior to the service Jesus performed?

What was the service that Jesus rendered?

Was this particular service His responsibility?

Was Jesus asked to serve? Read John 13:4.

Describe the job Jesus did. Was it glamorous? Prestigious? Desirable?

What service are you too proud to do?

What service are you too proud to receive?

Have you refrained from service because no one has asked you to serve?

How would you have spent your time if you had been facing execution the following day?

SERVICE OFFERED OBEDIENTLY — John 13:12 – 16

What are two reasons Jesus gives for your service? See John 13:12 – 16.

Give other reasons for service from 1 Corinthians 6:20; 2 Corinthians 5:14 – 15; Ephesians 6:6 – 7; 1 Timothy 6:1 – 2; Hebrews 13:11 – 16; 1 Peter 4:8 – 11; Revelation 1:6.

How does your obedient service reflect His? See Philippians 2:1 – 8.

SERVICE OFFERED GLADLY — John 13:17

What does Jesus say will be the result of your loving, willing, humble, obedient service to Him?

From John 13:17?

From John 12:26?

From 2 Corinthians 4:1, 7, 16 – 18?

My attic holds many things that were given to me as gifts — things that were lovingly, carefully, thoughtfully selected, but that I don't want and have no use for. I wonder how many of our "gifts" are in the King's attic? This year, celebrate Christmas by giving the King of Kings a gift He wants!

The Magnificent Obsession

Embracing the God-Filled Life

Anne Graham Lotz

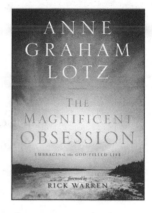

God longs to call you friend.

Are you missing the essentials to living a joyful, purpose-filled life? Are you devoted to your church or your religion but still struggling to find meaning and passion in your faith? Do you love your family, work hard, contribute to your community, but still feel your life is somehow incomplete and hollow at the core? Are you restless in your spirit, with a nagging sense that there must be something more?

Gifted Bible teacher Anne Graham Lotz, daughter of evangelist Billy Graham, has known this struggle herself. As she studied Scripture looking for a way out of the emptiness, she found her answer in the amazing story of Abraham, a very ordinary man who became extraordinary for one pivotal reason: he pursued God in a life of obedient faith, not knowing where that decision would take him. Despite struggling, as we do, with compromise, fear, family, quarrels, failure, doubt, and disappointment, Abraham became a man God called His friend.

Anne followed Abraham's lead and began a lifelong pursuit of knowing God, as he truly is, in an intensely personal relationship. Through personal anecdotes, unforgettable stories, and God-inspired insights, she invites you to draw closer to God, who is as committed to you as he was to Abraham and longs to call you friend.

Hardcover, Jacketed: 978-0-310-26288-6

Pick up a copy at your favorite bookstore or online!

ZONDERVAN®
.com

A Note to the Reader

After completing this devotional, if you need additional resources to help you dig deeper into God's Word, please contact Anne Graham Lotz through one of the following means:

AnGeL Ministries
5115 Hollyridge Drive
Raleigh, North Carolina 27612
919.787.6606
www.AnneGrahamLotz.com.
angelmin.info@angelministries.org

We want to hear from you. Please send your comments about this book to us in care of zreview@zondervan.com. Thank you.

ZONDERVAN.com/
AUTHORTRACKER
follow your favorite authors